With Revolutionary ♥

JADA MONICA DREW

CREATIVE LEADERSHIP & ACTION FOR SOCIAL CHANGE

REVOLUTIONIZE
NOW

REVOLUTIONIZE NOW
Copyright © 2016 by Jada Monica Drew
All rights reserved.

Printed Book- ISBN: 978-0-9974333-0-2

Book design by KPE Media

Published and printed in the United States by Social Designs
www.socialdesignsconsulting.com

First Edition

For
Watson Drew, Jr.
My Daddy. My Revolutionary.

Joanne Phillips Drew
My Mommy. My Revolutionary.

The 252.
My Heritage. My Ancestors. My Revolutionaries.

CONTENTS

FROM JADA, WITH LOVE.

I am powerful.
I am a hard worker.
I am a daughter, aunt, niece, sister, & friend.
I am beautiful.
I have favor over my life.
I am capable of doing any and everything I ever dreamed.
I am blessed.
I am self-conscious.
I am privileged.
I am loved.
I am a revolutionary because I know all of these things.

Today in my 30-year-old body I am all of the above, but I didn't always believe in my power and capabilities. I didn't always believe I was beautiful and my understanding of privilege and power didn't exist. That said, I definitely didn't consider myself a revolutionary. My developmental years are rooted in Rich Square, North Carolina, a small town of a little less than 1000 in population. My childhood home was a palace that my Daddy built. Our house was in the middle of two dirt roads with a paved cul-de-sac. On each side and behind the house were long-leaf pine trees encasing the house. On the left was a basketball goal and the right, a sandbox and in-ground pool. In front was a blue and white swing set next to a huge sci-fi- like solar panel. All around the yard there were beautiful flowers and sculptures.

On the weekends and on holidays, my childhood home was the party house. Either my parents had 'get-togethers' with family or I was hosting a festive holiday party or sleepover. I always loved connecting and hosting people, and having a good time. Life as a child and teenager was fairly easy and celebratory, although there were painful moments that went beyond scarred knees, such as dealing with the deaths of loved ones and other family tragedies.

I was sheltered from the experiences of hunger, homelessness, poverty, and crime, but at the early age of 12, I started to become more 'woke.' My parents committed to reminding me that I was fortunate and some people in this world suffered unnecessarily. Anytime my parents felt like I was 'smelling myself' or in other words, ungrateful and acting out with an arrogant attitude; I was quickly put in my place. I remember once as a teenager my Daddy told me that God could easily take away all of my blessings as quick as I could blink my eyes. My mom always taught me to be nice to people no matter what because you never know what someone is going through. Through their teachings, fun-loving and hilarious personalities, respect for elders, love for 'the 252,' and strong work ethic, I became Jada Monica Drew.

My parents are revolutionaries. My Mom sets an example for many in her family through her love for education and her loyalty and dedication to give back. My Daddy literally built communities and created jobs. They both are the realist, most humble, and hilarious people I know. I learned from them how to be revolutionary. I learned from my parents the power of being unique, sacrificing yourself for others, and inspiring others to be the best they can be. My mom taught me the power of being present and serving others just by listening to their stories, while my dad taught me about the power that develops when people work together for a common goal.

REVOLUTIONIZE NOW TERMINOLOGY

Revolutionize Now is written in standardized United States English and slang. In the process of writing, it has been important for me to proudly acknowledge my language as a tool for resistance. I celebrate linguistic variety while writing, presenting, and teaching. Throughout this book you will experience and learn from my culture through language. An explanation of terms that are '_____' can be found below.

Across the way – across the street, down the road, or other side of town

Africana CHANGE- Founded by Jada Drew, the mission of the collegiate, high school, and youth program is to empower youth and young adults by providing cultural, artistic, and educational programming, and to support them in developing their success as they become driven global leaders who understand the value of respect, the importance of social justice, and the power of celebrating the Black Diaspora.

Principles
C Character Development
H Heritage Awareness
A Academic Excellence
N Nourishment
G Global Leadership
E Enrichment & Exposure

Black Community – a generic term used to describe people of African descent; can be problematic because not all Black people identify the same or believe in the same values; in the context of the book the community that is most affected

Black Girl Magic – a term used to illustrate the universal awesomeness of Black Women. It's about celebrating anything we deem particularly dope, inspiring, or mind-blowing about ourselves.

Black Wallsteets – prominent communities around the United States where Black people owned businesses, and held political power.

Calling out – speak out against what someone is saying; to hold accountable

Code-switching – the ability to change your dialect or languages while communicating; survival mechanism

Crack jokes – to tell a series of funny stories or anecdotes with or about someone

Cut Up – to have a fabulous time

Dopeness – awesome and amazing, unique

Good liberal people – individuals who work hard to be good change agent oftentimes lacking a full awareness of their power and privilege

Get-togethers – gathering of people usually involving food, laughter, and drinks

Going natural – the process of extracting chemicals from your hair

Internalized Oppression – self-criticism, self-hate, mistrust of people who share same identities based on negative stereotypes

Keisha and Diana – the names I give to my wigs

Knock out drag out – heated argument, or physical altercation

Lay the sides – 1- partial relaxer 2- slick the edges of your hair with products for the purpose of laying flat; preferably with a tooth brush and edge control

Naps – naturally tightly curled or coiled hair

Paper bag test – when a brown paper bag is compared to a Black person's face to determine if you were granted access to certain privileges, social clubs, or churches

Pisstivity – highly pissed off, upset and angry

Putting you in your place – to humble a person

Reading you – the act of correcting someone in a witty and snarky manner

Shoot the "ish" – chatting; gossiping, having conversation

Smelling myself – feeling highly of yourself, conceited

Stay out of your feelings – avoid being emotional and over exaggerating

Sugarcoat – to make the truth sound less harsh; telling half-truths; beating around the bush

That thing – strongly describing something

The 252 – referring to northeastern North Carolina culture; the numbers refer to the area code

Tight – 1- closeness, 2- amazing, 3- mad or angry

Time out – the moment to cease something; take a break or pause

Woke – to be conscious about systems of oppression and empowerment movements

INTRODUCTION

The purpose of Revolutionize Now is to ignite the creative leader and revolutionary in you. Yes, you are a revolutionary. Revolutionaries re-imagine systems, they protest, they deny injustice, they create works of art, they shift their mindsets, they build, they research, they challenge, they empower, and they inspire. The most clever revolutionaries and creative leaders have used countless versions of resisting and revolting.

Resist: to push away from something undesired or unhealthy.

Revolt: to escape from bondage and rise up, oftentimes against governed authority; mental enlightenment.

I used to think that activism and revolution looked like protesting and war, but revolution is multifaceted. It has to be. Think about it. If we live in a multi-layered society, shouldn't social change occur in multiple ways? Living in such complex societies merits multiple levels of revolution.

In 2013, the Black Lives Matter Movement sparked a flame inside of me. Young Black Queer leaders started a hashtag and organizing efforts that propelled communities around the world to stand up for Black liberation. Hundreds of thousands of protesters organized highway take-overs, rallies, and town hall meetings. This began a different wave of youth movement building. The nation and the world demanded there be justice, accountability, and strategy to end systemic racism.

During this time, I asked myself, "What is my role?" My role as an educator is to revolutionize by continuing to inspire youth and college students to strive for excellence AND rethink a new path for social justice. As a consultant and trainer, I'm determined to work with leaders who have decision making power and equip them with tools to transform systems, imagine innovative ways for social change, and accept personal accountability.

This book is written as a guide with very clear steps for revolutionaries who are doing radical work and for budding revolutionaries who are looking to embark on a social justice journey. I define Revolutionize Now as:

REVOLUTIONIZE:
To radically change something, someone, or a system. A different way of thinking, doing, and being.
• •

NOW:
Immediately, urgently, timely; moving with the spirit and goal of here and now.
• •

REVOLUTIONIZE NOW:
Actualizing your power to reframe your mindset in order to radically change with a spirit of urgency.
• •

This book embraces my professional experiences in higher education, non-profit, government, and private sectors; as well as my growth as a woman, my love of people, and my understandings within a global context. My challenges and failures continue to mold me into a better person and leader. There have been tons of mistakes or more so learning moments in my career thus far. There has been much celebration as well. All of my experiences paint a picture that is a masterpiece; messy, disjointed, and ever-evolving. I consider myself a budding revolutionary with so much more to learn.

Ever since my college days, work as a social justice activist has been rewarding, successful, yet frustrating as hell. I often notice very small and simple road blocks that can be avoided if people get out of their own way. I'm in the room with decision makers who make tons of excuses to avoid accountability and slow the process toward social change. I am in community with constituents, students, workers, and community members who need to see the change now!

In understanding my personal and our collective power to revolutionize, it is mandatory that I ask myself "how can I be better and how am I contributing to the problem?" In order to access my personal power, I must realize that to be a part of the solution, I must also be aware of my power and privilege. As social justice activists, we need to be aware of our unconscious bias and the ways we are socialized to perpetuate oppression.

For example, sometimes...

I am judgmental.

I am rude.

I am classist.

I am cist gender.
I am defensive.
I am prejudice.
I am human.
I am a revolutionary because I know all of these things.

Radical community change is possible if we all understand our power, privilege, and ways that we have been oppressed. Realizing our collective truth as a tool for social change will get us closer to a more socially just world. At this moment in United States history, we are battling with the realization that we need systems and we simultaneously experience brutal impacts of existing systems. Often times, social change agents do not acknowledge our own privileges and how those privileges are sources of the very problems that we are fighting against. This is one reason why reflection is key. As Lauryn Hill states in the song, "Mr. Intentional",

"We are stuck in a system that seeks to suck your blood. Held emotionally hostage by what everybody does. Exploiting ignorance in the name of love...Stop before you drop because that's just the way it was. Please don't justify me, Mr. Intentional. Wake up you've been sleeping." [3]

Social change starts with an individual waking up and staying 'woke'. After the awakening, we can tackle the house (family & friends), the local, the nation, and the globe. Revolutionize Now is a self-care and transformational guide for individuals who are in need of different ways to approach organizations, people, and movement building. The goal is to create more inclusivity and equity within the systems we all utilize or to tear it up and rebuild. After reading

Revolutionize Now, I hope that you will be more equipped with a magic armor of courage, confidence, strategy, and love.

I'm offering you these three things that are critical in doing social justice work and will help you become a revolutionary too; Historic Truth-Telling, Building Relationships, and Creative Action. These components guide the work of Social Designs.

HISTORIC TRUTH-TELLING

HISTORIC: Looking back into how the world came to be and how societies were formed. Each person is connected to history, ancestors, major events, institutions, policy, culture, movements, tragedy, and triumph. TRUTH-TELLING: sharing your truth and experiences with a group of people. Truth-telling also means hearing about how your impact towards others has an effect. Sometimes your impact does not always match your intent and you may be doing more harm than good. When we are open to creating an environment of responsible historic truth-telling we can understand and support each other from a place of trust.

BUILDING RELATIONSHIPS

BUILDING RELATIONSHIPS: To build relationships is to decide who you are and how you really want to connect with others. Connecting with others in a meaningful, deep, and spiritual way is powerful. There is beauty in collective power and action. Creating the action requires trust. I must trust you to do the work well. I may not agree with your process or philosophy, but if the long-term goal is social change for the greater good then we can be in community. How can I trust you if I don't know you or if we haven't developed a relationship where we can respectfully disagree? When you build relationships you are building deeper connections that are rooted in radical love and not surface existence.

CREATIVE ACTION

CREATIVE ACTION: Creativity ignites energy you never knew existed. When I am tapping into my creative side alone or with others I feel free and my mind is clearer. If we are seeking social change, creativity must be a part of the process. I polled a group of students in a Community Problem Solving course that I am teaching at a local college. The question was, "Do you feel like you have the power to change the state of the world?" The majority of these energetic, creative, witty, and intelligent students responded with a very solid "no." My heart dropped. Through continued inquiry, I learned that they did not feel powerful because they did not have much faith in our current political system and other systems. Immediately, the prepared lesson plan went out of the window and we then collectively explored the question, "What can we do to revolutionize now and change systems?" Some of the responses included voting, initiative, sacrifice, influence, action, and changing mindsets. I am inspired to continue to create space for our present and our future generations to be in constant inquiry of ways to revolutionize.

When I set out to write this book, I was anxious to share my heart, my ideas, and my journey. Along the way, I would think to myself, "But maybe I should wait. Maybe I need to read more and do more before I tell the people what I think about social change." I thought what I had to share just was not good enough yet. Then I started to think about the people I have impacted. I started to think about those who seek my advice. I started to think about my purpose. I know that my purpose is to build communities. I began to visualize all of the amazing communities all over the world who have welcomed me and taught me so much and how I've paid the knowledge forward. During daily meditation time on a cold sunny day in my cloud, (that's the meditation and creativity room in my home), a memory came to me. This memory was of young women who shared testimonies of how in a short span of 6 months to 4 years, I was able to help spark a light in them that exuded excellence, inner & outer beauty, power, and courage. I was humbled and amazed at how much God was able to use me. When I opened my eyes, I said to myself. It is time. It is time to strike that spark, just a bit harder and to illuminate that flame much wider.

I want to celebrate the good in us all. I want to move people to ignite their creative leadership and power. I want to be a catalyst for sustainable, healthy, and prosperous change. It is time out for business as usual. If leaders continue to operate in the same way within the same systems of inequity, nothing will change. I've seen too many people suffer at the hands

of those who are in privileged spaces. I have seen and felt
the tears of thousands of college students who furiously fight
for justice within the very walls of institutions who they pay
thousands of dollars to yearly. I have seen small differences
tear up friendships, families, and communities because people lack the skills to get through tough conversations. Yearly,
with a team of well-skilled facilitators, I mobilize 500 middle
and high school students at the national Youth Action Project
of the White Privilege Conference and hear the pain and fearless hope in their hearts. I speak to employees who are seeking well-deserved acknowledgement and to simply be treated
fairly. I have also seen students rise up and demand for equal
rights on college campuses; youth organize and bring difficult
and meaningful conversations to schools nationwide; and
employees in service industries, faculty, and Fortune 500 staff
build internal resources to support affinity and equity initiatives. These examples illustrate the power and the tools that
we have to revolutionize now.

It is time.

It is time to Revolutionize Now!

CREATIVE
LEADERSHIP
BEGINS
WITHIN

1

REACH BACK
"SANKOFA"

"The concept of SANKOFA is derived from King Adinkra of the Akan people of West Africa. SANKOFA is expressed in the Akan language as "se wo were fi na wosan kofa a yenki." Literally translated it means "it is not taboo to go back and fetch what you forgot". "Sankofa" teaches us that we must go back to our roots in order to move forward. That is, we should reach back and gather the best of what our past has to teach us, so that we can achieve our full potential as we move forward. Whatever we have lost, forgotten, forgone or been stripped of, can be reclaimed, revived, preserved and perpetuated." [7]

When I was a little girl, my mom and dad would take me around to visit family on Saturdays and Sundays. There was a list of folks were determined to see.. One of my favorite places to visit was Lovers Lane. The unique thing about Lovers Lane is that in almost all of the homes there lived a couple and each couple was related to the next, somehow. The couples included, Nanny & Duke, Rachel & Snook, Uncle Jabo and Aunt Bert, Aunt Lizzy and Boot Jack, Vernell and PeeWee, Daisy & Bob, Mildred and June, Velma & Pook; and many more. The children and grandchildren of Lovers Lane built a bond that we still have to this day. Our bond is connected like the strong threads connecting a hand-woven quilt. Like quilts, our stories and lessons from elders paints a beautiful tapestry of life, love, and loyalty. On Lovers Lane, we learned to have each other's back. As the baby of the crew, I was spoiled and protected by my older cousins. We learned to support each other. None of us youth, the 30-40 somethings, live on Lovers Lane anymore nor do any of our parents or grandparents. However, we come home frequently and support the younger generation. We also know how to get together to celebrate life and our accomplishments. And when we party, we party hard.

Up the road a bit we would visit my maternal Grandma Virginia and Granddaddy Edwin. At their house we would also see my Uncle Jerome who taught me patience, how to play basketball, and how to tie my shoes among many other things. Across the street we would visit Shoke (Pauline) and her family. My paternal Grandma MaMaggie's house was a stop as well. We would walk "across the way" to see Uncle Coy and Aunt Janice, and down the road to see Uncle Charles and Aunt Debbie. Usually Uncle Coy would make his way to our house early on Sunday mornings to 'shoot the ish' with my Daddy and to 'crack jokes' with my Mom.

During these visits I would learn so much by listening and watching. The elders would always share their wisdom. I can remember my Uncle Coy telling me to work hard and never forget where I came from. He was key in telling me to always be thankful for what I have and to take nothing but top notch from people pursuing me. I remember how Nanny's house had a revolving door. People were always there. She baked the best cakes and made the best collard greens. I learned from

Nanny the importance of just loving on people, being inviting, and keeping it real. Nanny kept it real at all times.

Where I'm from and who my people are has shaped me into the woman I am today. I exude loyalty, hospitality, sincerity, and a love for people. My father taught me to always give back to my community and to help people. He also made it a point to acknowledge the greatness I came from and also the struggle. His grandfather owned a brick company and his grandfather's father purchased many acres of land when it was unthinkable for a Black man to do so in the late 1800s. After purchasing the land, he made it a point to sell the land back to his family and community members. When returning from New York as a business man, my Daddy did the same thing in the 1970s and 80s. He bought land, built houses, and worked with the banks himself to finance the homes for people in the community. They were revolutionary by adding to the economic sustainability of Black people in Rich Square, NC and surrounding areas in Northeastern, NC.

Returning With A Spirit Of Excellence

While hanging out with my grandparents and elders and their friends, I would learn so much about how the town I am from used to have so many Black businesses and so much community love. I want us to return to this spirit of excellence. What's missing is the Sankofa knowledge of what already existed before. This place was once where jobs and economic sustainability was more of a reality. Even though my home county, Northampton County is one of the poorest in the state, in the past people were able to sustain themselves and there was a great deal of self-employed people. What stopped this spirit from growing? Many things got in the way like people moving away, big business, and changes in the schools. We should take time to dissect what happened to inform next steps for social change. Equally important, we must also move into creative action.

Creative Leadership: So Fresh & So Green Project

In 2011, with the guidance and support of the non-profit founded by Van Jones, I launched the 252 Revitalization Project (now the So Fresh & So Green Project) with family in Rich Square to get back to this spirit of excellence. Our main goal was to use the principles of environmental justice and sustainability as a platform for economic growth and creative action. After five years, the project has evolved. We work with 100 – 200 youth from the ages of 10 to 18. The concepts taught in Rich Square, from hospitality to love, are present in our project. The next step is to embed more sustainable and collective action. We used what we learned from our elders and poured it into the lives of the youth. Now a program that started off as a community sustainability awareness and clean-up effort has blossomed into an annual school assembly, awards ceremony, and annual international trip to Barbados for youth.

Just as much as I have learned from my elders in my hometown of Rich Square, I have learned from mentors and elders in many working environments. I believe that you must listen to the stories of those who have been a part of the system in order to create change. Even though I honor the wisdom of many elders in my communities, I will be honest and say that the young Jada (still young Jada ☺) would wonder, "Why don't we just make a change now? Why can't we do things faster? Why can't we just tell people exactly how we feel and how we see things?" I would think that the methods of my mentors or elders were too slow and not rooted in urgency. What I have learned over the years is that urgency for social change looks different for every community, organization, and person. My mentors and elders taught me that creative leadership and innovation is possible when you are equipped to tell and take the truth and when you are flexible enough to utilize multiple tactics for social change.

Follow the 2 T's.

1. Truth-telling

2. Tactics

TRUTH-TELLING – The truth will set you free.

Truth-telling is one of the principles of Social Designs. When working with groups of people within organizations I always stress the importance of historic truth telling. Truth propels us to understand each other from a deep level of spirit and humanity. When working to commemorate the 50th anniversary of Black integration at Guilford College, I had the honor and privilege of hearing so many truths from my elders. I learned first-hand about the experiences of the first Black students and first Black tenured professors. James McMillian, James McCorkle, Dr. Adrienne Israel, Dr. Edwins Gwako, Carolyn Beard Whitlow, Barbara Lawrence, Dr. Karen Tinsley, Dr. Karen Hayes, Dr. Minnette Coleman, and Ruth Watakila were among the firsts whom I had the honor to get to know and learn from directly. There were countless of others stories of many other alumni and "firsts" at the College. What I uncovered in their truths were perspectives that were not always publicized as the norm.

Their truths helped me to understand more deeply why certain things at the College were still present and to fully comprehend my role from a historical perspective as the Multicultural Education Department Director. The equity and inclusion work was informed by their heartfelt and transparent stories. Their truths also further developed a strong sense of pride and admiration for the place where I spent the majority of my day. I value the moments when I can learn from people who have done it before. In troubling times like today in a very pivotal moment in US and world history, we must learn from our past to inform our future. If we don't many of ills of society and institutions will reappear.

We must uncover the stories of our elders to learn from the past so that we do not allow the systemic damning of our humanity to continue. We must wake up! Waking up helps us to understand what is going on in our society and also includes learning from the past. We cannot be so beside ourselves to ignore the wisdom and guidance of our mentors and elders when seeking social change.

Who are the respected leaders with "status" in your community? What is their story in relationship to community activism?

_____

_____

_____

_____

Who are the respected elders and leaders with power? What is their story in relationship to community activism?

_____

_____

_____

_____

Who are your mentors and elders? What can you ask them in order to gain a deeper understanding of your community?

_____

_____

_____

_____

TACTICS – Strategic revolution creates sustainable change.

While a young leader in the field of higher education, I led a presentation for upper leadership and board members of the college. My presentation was about ways the VPs could support and lead in an effort to celebrate diversity and racial equity. The presentation was well-organized, concise, and in short, bad-ass. I can remember the painful silence in the room afterwards. No one had questions, concerns, ideas, or criticisms. I was appalled at how withdrawn this group of leaders who claimed to honor diversity were from of actualizing it, breathing it, or at least wanting to be curious. I was heated and pissed off for so many reasons. One reason is the time it took me to complete the presentation with compiling data and fact checking. Another reason is because my time could have been spent doing something else that directly supporting students.

After the meeting, I met with a few elders to share my frustration and my plan to be direct in asking those in the meeting, "Why is there a perceived lack of concern for diversity by the evident silence?" My mentor looked at me, smiled, and simply said that there's always a way to get what you want. You just have to strategize. Next we sat and planned for about an hour on how to maneuver through the system at hand with grace, tact, and authenticity. At first, I was not trying to listen and felt a sense of urgency. Then I remembered what my Daddy used to always tell me. "Always listen to old-folk or those older than you. They have been here before and have seen more than you." So I listened. When approaching the same group of leaders, my approach was slightly different as well as my results. At the next meeting, there was more engagement, questions, and interaction.

Take a closer look at how you approach problems.

What is your primary tactic in being a revolutionary? Why do you approach problems this way?

_____

_____

_____

_____

_____

_____

What tactics do you appreciate the most? What tactics are most challenging for you?

_____

_____

_____

_____

What are the three tactics you have seen the most utilized in your community or organization for social change?

_____

_____

_____

_____

Organize your tactics according to areas of the community or organization.

Tactics	Who leads the strategy?	Who is Affected by it?	Why is this Tactic chosen?
1.			
2.			
3.			

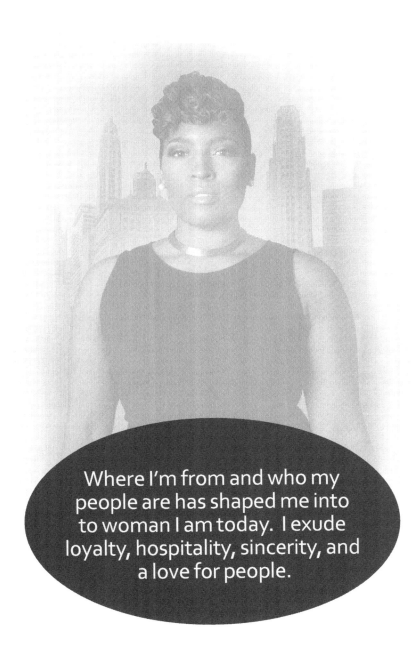

Where I'm from and who my people are has shaped me into to woman I am today. I exude loyalty, hospitality, sincerity, and a love for people.

2

MAGIC

#BlackGirlMagic: a term used to illustrate the universal awesomeness of Black Women. It's about celebrating anything we deem particularly dope, inspiring, or mind-blowing about ourselves.[9]

One of my favorite quotes is by Ruby Dee Davis. Mrs. Davis stated, "Life is not a trajectory, I am always becoming," as she accepted the living legend award at the 2010 Black Girls Rock Awards Show. There is magic in knowing that I can constantly evolve in life if I so choose. In that moment, a light bulb turned on in my head! Mrs. Ruby Dee reminded me that I must continuously seek to enjoy life, to make my life worth living, thrive, and become whatever it was I wanted to be.

I was 24 when Ms. Ruby Dee spoke to my spirit, during that time I was entering into a season of actualizing my full potential in life. The trajectory I was on was one of living out my #BlackGirlMagic. I was at a pivotal moment in my career and my womanhood. This discovery of finding my magic, womanhood, and Blackness was deeply embedded in a history and reality of self-doubt. As a Black woman, I consciously and subconsciously experience the effects of colorism and sexism.

The hierarchy of skin tone and hair texture has deeply influenced my entire life. While growing up in Northampton County, I had about five solid girlfriends. We did everything together. As early as 4th grade, I noticed that the girls in my little crew who got the attention from the boys or the compliments from the teachers were the girls with light skin and straight hair. Because I'm on the cusp of brown skin, (self-identified pecan brown) I generally felt that I was treated well because I was not considered dark skinned, yet I did notice the overwhelming attention towards light skinned girls. I remember how all of us would 'crack jokes' about each other depending on our complexion, and some of the jokes were quite brutal. Studies show that children as early as four years are exposed to messages that influence bias based on skin complexion and other socially created markers of race. We were getting these messages from our parents, television, magazines, and other youth.

BLACK WOMAN HAIR & COMPLEXION

Zora Neale Hurston, an author, anthropologist and revolutionary who added an unprecedented amount of value to Black dialects in the United States conducted early 19th century studies which documented how, 'the Black Community,' categorized hair texture and skin tone throughout that time period. Unfortunately, those issues are still prevalent today. Hurston wrote about real issues and tragedies, when the norm during the Harlem Renaissance was to write about the advancement of colored people and how "cultured" we were. When I first read her book, Speak, So You Can Speak Again: The Life of Zora Neale Hurston4, I was inspired to look more deeply at how the concepts of "good" and "bad" are so deeply entrenched within our collective psyche. Engaging these types of binaries brought me to a place where I wanted to see them applied as a point of learning about and, in some ways, unlearning this way of thinking. I shared these descriptors (good and bad) with Africana CHANGE students and through reflection sessions, we began to share our "good hair, bad hair," "light skinned, dark skinned" stories. This challenged us to uncover deep and traumatic memories.

From the Harlem Slanguages of Hurston's book,

- GOOD HAIR, Caucasian-type hair
- BAD HAIR, Negro-type hair
- RIGHTEOUS MOSS OR GRASS, good hair
- NEARER MY GOD TO THEE, good hair
- NAPS, kinky hair
- MADE HAIR, hair that has been straightened
- TIGHT HEAD, one with kinky hair
- EVERY POSTMAN ON HIS BEAT, kinky hair
- COAL SCUTTLE BLONDE, black hair
- PINK TOES, yellow girl
- COLOR SCALE:
  o High yaller
  o Yaller
  o High Brown
  o Vaseline brown
  o Seal brown
  o Low brown
  o Dark brown

For generations, there has been an unhealthy reality about complexion and colorism in the community. I believe some of the root causes are the economic and psychological system of slavery, color based classism, and the intentional division of the African Diaspora. The effect that it had on me was negative. I didn't think I was pretty enough. Even though my hair was long (and long was considered desirable), I felt my hair was too thick and I remember the day I finally got a relaxer. I was so happy that I didn't need the straightening comb anymore and that my mom did not have to struggle with my 'naps.' I viewed myself as more feminine, more accepted and more beautiful. When thinking back to how detrimental those moments were, I get teary eyed. Why do we put ourselves and our daughters through a process that literally strips them from their natural being? There is psychological warfare happening.

Now, don't get me wrong. I'm not saying that if you get a relaxer or weave that you are less authentic. Every month I have an appointment to 'lay the sides' of my short cut. What I am saying is that when we do not allow our young girls to love their natural hair to the point where they do not know what their natural hair feels like as an adult, we have to examine *why*. We also have to examine why we are so harsh with each other when it comes to different skin tones. We assign stereotypes to ourselves based on color complexion. This is prevalent in fraternities and paternities, the historic 'paper bag tests,' and in the current #TeamLightSkin versus #TeamDarkSkin debate among our youth. We have to examine and talk about it. The day we begin to uncover our collective histories of pain, will be the day we heal.

As for me, I have evolved. I love my natural hair. I love my short and modern relaxed style. I like color additions. I like braid extensions. I like my 'Keisha and Diana' (I name my wigs). Versatility is fun and stylish. However, I am in a place now where I love myself whether I'm rocking my big nappy poof or my relaxed sassy cut. It is revolutionary to get to a place of loving who you are holistically. As a Black woman, this is not always easy. Luckily, there are more positive and versatile images of Black women in mainstream media outlets that reflect reality.

BLACK WOMAN BOSS BUSINESS

My Black Girl Magic did not come into full effect immediately. It was a journey that was painful, yet liberating. I began working in higher education very young. I was fierce and fearless. I was confident with my intelligence and ready to begin my career and be successful. However, early on I battled with outside forces and messages that would constantly communicate, "Don't be too Black, or you will scare the White people. Don't be too emotional or passionate or you will be seen as a weak woman. Don't dress this way, because you will seem too young or too sexual." These messages were exhausting to hear each day as I put on my attitude and attire for the day. Even if the thoughts were only for a split second or a minute, it was draining contemplating my wardrobe. It was tiresome trying not to sound like my Southern, witty, and charismatic self. 'Code-switching' and navigating spaces was aggravating as hell. And honestly, many times I did not know this dance was happening. It became my new normal. I would make sure not to exude the characteristics of the stereotypical angry Black woman (even when I *was* angry) during difficult conversations or when I was passionate about supporting students or passionate about calling out occurrences of bias and discrimination within the departments of the College.

Additionally, I even paid close attention to my hair styles during certain meetings. I could go from a close cut Caesar fade, to a fro-hawk, to a large afro, to a straightened look. Through these changes of hair styles, it was amazing how compliments would come flushing in when my hair was more European looking or straight vs. Afro-centric. One of my White male colleagues, who I respect dearly, and I were in a meeting one day with a group of staff and faculty members who were working to implement anti-racist and inclusion policies at the college. On this day, I was wearing a very fly business suit and my hair was in two-strand twists (an Afrocentric style). We all had a great meeting. The next day, I was in another meeting with some of the same people, including my respected White male colleague, and I wore jeans, a dress shirt, pumps and my hair had been straightened. My colleague complimented me by saying, "You look very nice today." My response was "Thank you. What's different between yesterday and today?" Before he could respond, I said, my hair is straight, hmmm." Now, this man didn't mean any harm by complimenting me. He was being nice. Right? Of course. However, being in my skin, this micro aggression was very present and it had a long-lasting effect on me. Now the funny and simultaneously disturbing thing about this story to note, is that I have had this experience with people of color as well (see internalized racial oppression in glossary).

Straight hair, good hair, nappy hair, bad hair. This is a conversation I have with friends and family often. Formal and informal dialogue about colorism dates back for at least a century, as aforementioned in Hurston's categories. In our inner circles we talk about whether relaxers are bad or not. We discuss the maintenance of natural hair. Women share hair serum secrets and tips for the 'going natural process' (Isn't it ironic that we call it going natural?). Just as I mentioned the reaction of my white colleague in response to my straight hair, there are Black responses to natural hair and this happens interracially as well. Because I have done almost everything with my hair, the stories are endless. When my hair is obviously natural and I walk into an "afro-centric" store or event, I get a lot of "How ya doing my sista" and "Beautiful hair queen." On both spectrums, I appreciate the response, but what's funny about the responses is the way it changes depending on the audience and the texture of my hair.

The hair decisions, conversations, and contemplations take up a lot of time and space. It has become a part of my life. I hope that when my children are born, this conversation will be over and they will fully accept and celebrate their hair as it is, along with the rest of the world.

To make the world better for generations to come, we have to start with action now. In my profession I realized that no matter what I did or didn't do to my hair, my language, and appearance it was inevitable that I would receive comments and go through emotional and psychological cycles. So I said "F" it! I might as well do what I want to do with pride, class, and 'dopeness'! Luckily I was employed in a multicultural affairs office. My supervisor was also very supportive in identity expression as she was a conscious Black woman. However, I took this spirt with me into board meetings, consultations with clients, trainings with corporate partners, and workshops with youth. And guess what? I am always complimented on my style and my hair. Because I know that I am bold and beautiful, everyone else has no other choice but to accept me and celebrate me as I am. This is just one account of how I began the journey to find my #BlackGirlMagic.

Living in this pecan brown skin is a blessing. Yet living behind these deep dark brown eyes offers a perspective that is beautiful and painstakingly amazing. I'm still uncovering and discovering magic daily. On every occasion I get, I make it a point to say out loud through my personality and the way I communicate that my ethnicity, gender identity, race, and intelligence are magical. I make it a point to simply be me, unapologetically. I also make a point to compliment, support, and love on all women. **This is Revolutionary Black Girl Magic.**

Explore your magic! Take a moment to write down what it is that you love or appreciate about your…

Intelligence:

_____

_____

Culture:

_____

_____

Race/Ethnicity:

_____

_____

Hobbies/Talents:

_____

_____

Gender Identity:

_____

_____

Skin:

_____

_____

Hair:

_____

_____

Body:

_____

_____

My Black girl magic did not come into full effect immediately. It was a journey that was painful, yet liberating.

3

LIVE OUT LOUD, UNAPOLOGETICALLY

I live out loud, unapologetically. Why? I'm not ok with the status quo or with fitting into the boxes created for young Black women. I say these things aloud to affirm myself and to give women like me permission to celebrate themselves and the life that is purposed for them. In retrospect, there are so many reasons why I should not live out loud; doubt and chastisement have come to me from people who were supposed to be supportive. Just as I've had to find my Black Girl Magic, I've had to make the decision to be unapologetically me. One might ask how I got to this place of affirmation. I would say trial and error, faith in my purpose to build communities, and the desire to LIVE OUT LOUD.

INTERRUPTIONS OF LIVING OUT LOUD

Middle School

In middle school, I was a happy child and was involved in everything. I played basketball, acted in school theatre, and played the trumpet in the band. One afternoon in band practice, I was laughing and joking around with friends. For a reason that I cannot recall, the band teacher came to me and said that I needed to be careful of having too much confidence because it might get me in trouble one day. My 12-year-old self was confused and shocked. I didn't understand why a grown up would tell me not to be confident. At that moment I felt silenced. Sadly, his comments were a permanent voice in my head throughout high school and affected my self-esteem and confidence at times.

The King Campaign

In college a group of young women and I worked tirelessly to lead a campaign to celebrate our Black male peers who were doing positive things in the community, yet stereotyped as uneducated, violent and invisible. The name of the movement was The King Campaign. We organized a rally, appeared on local television and radio stations, and were on everyone's Facebook feed in its inaugural years; before hashtags. The t-shirt with the message, "I Still Love Black Men," sold like hotcakes and we used the profits to tour in NC, VA, GA, and Tennessee. With all of the positivity that came out of this national effort, there was local pushback from elders. We were told that our message would be sensualized and sexualized because we were women supporting men. We were led to believe that people were sincerely there to support us. But in the long run, they wanted power to generate similar messages. We felt let down by the disgrace and disloyalty from people who presented themselves as helpful.

My First Job

Fresh out of college, I worked in collaboration with AmeriCorps VISTA (Volunteers in Service to America) and the Student to Student Literacy program of the University of Chapel Hill on a literacy campaign. AmeriCorps VISTA is a national service program created to fight poverty in the United States of America. My job was to partner with two local schools and increase the literacy levels of the youth selected for the program. This position connected to my service learning, psychology, and education background and I was super excited. The only downside was that AmeriCorps paid minimum wage. After going to school for 4 years, equating to a $90,000 price tag, my family was not very supportive of a minimum wage job. They did not understand that I was following my passion and my purpose.

Regardless of those who didn't see God's vision for me, I gave myself permission to do things differently and to live out loud. I gave myself permission to make mistakes and love hard. To do this, I trusted my crazy ideas, surrounded myself with positive people who were not afraid to challenge me, and tapped into my creativity. I gave myself permission to be free.

MY CRAZY & CREATIVE IDEAS

Africana CHANGE – A Movement

One day after hosting a Black heritage conversation at a college, I was in deep dialogue with a professor about the similarities and differences among all Black people. My stance was that all Black people are more similar than we realize and most Black cultures carry deep African retentions. From that conversation, I asked my supervisor if I could start a program to help students of the African Diaspora explore their culture and heritage through research, travel, discussion, and community service. To my surprise, she said yes! Seven years later the Africana CHANGE (Character Development, Heritage Awareness, Nourishment, Global Leadership, Enrichment) program has evolved into a successful course of study at a predominately white institution, an in-school mentorship program at James B. Dudley High School, and an annual youth summit.   We were even able to make history as the first group of all Black students from the college to study abroad in Brazil. This one crazy idea that I had before even completing a masters has changed lives.   Hundreds of my peers, colleagues, and elders have played such an important role in the success of Africana CHANGE and Africana CHANGE Jr. The college students completing the program have all graduated and connected the principles of Africana CHANGE in their careers.   It has been a joy to see it grow and change lives!

A Little about the Program:

Africana CHANGE is such a unique program.   Before I began to create the program, I did extensive research to see what models were out there to insure that I was no recreating the wheel and supporting collective thinking. There was nothing like Africana CHANGE so I moved forward with planning.

This program is revolutionary because it was developed on the basis of popular education.   This means that we incorporated processes to empower the students by allowing them the space to co-design the curriculum. I put together a model that allowed constant reflection as it connected to important events, policies and cultural realms in history and today. Reflection came in the form of journaling, group conversations (in a circle) and assignments to spark their creativity. Importantly, each of the participants in these small classes represented the diversity of the African Diaspora. For example, we may have had a cluster of students encompassing: 1. A US born Jamaican woman with Immigrant parents living in the US, 2. A US born Nigerian American woman with an African American mother and Nigerian father, 3. A mixed race man who was Mexican and Black, and 4. A Black native woman who still lives on the land of her native ancestors. These individuals would then co-mold the curriculum based off of the identities in the room. It gave college students an opportunity to learn about the diversity of Africana people, the deep connections within those differences, and an opportunity to explore ancestry with resources. This is something that is not accessed by many Africana people.

The college course was designed with the participants, while the high school program involved constant input from the high school students in its continuously evolving design. When going into the high school, our college students learned about experiential learning facilitation by facilitating every 90-minute session. This model was designed to inspire trainers in those being trained. We all worked together to give our students and high schoolers the tools to challenge the status quo and to demand the best for their lives. We also included our elders in the process to vet the program and to share their stories and wisdom.

What is a crazy idea?

_____

_____

_____

_____

How is it revolutionary?

_____

_____

_____

_____

Who is the community that will stand with you to implement the program?

_____

_____

_____

_____

Who will your idea serve and why?

_____

_____

_____

Change Institute – An International Justice Collaboration

While studying global and international education, I was interested to connect more youth and students to global travel. I got this crazy idea to start a global travel and leadership program for youth. The first step was to further develop my skills. Secondly, I needed to recruit a supportive team of experts. Lastly, I made the program unique by adding as much of me into the design of the program as possible. That included: a holistic learning model, lots of fun, communal spaces, and an equity analysis. Essentially, everything I produce has to be unique and challenge the status quo.

Develop Your Skills. To build a successful study abroad program, I developed my skills by researching best practices for student pre-orientation methods and attended conferences to learn more about logistics and project management. What skills do you need to develop to grow your crazy idea and how will you develop each skill?

Skill	How will you develop your skill?
1.	
2.	
3.	

Recruit a Successful Team. I recruited a successful team by first acknowledging that I am not an expert in all things. I do not know everything and I am perfectly fine with needing help. This makes me successful in asking the right people for help when needed. Our first study abroad trip with youth was seamless because of the facilitators, logistical managers, and Bajan partners. Asking for help does not always mean that you should expect it for free. It means investing in those who invest in you.

What areas of expertise are needed to actualize your idea? Who can you call for help?

Expertise Area I:

_____

_____

_____

_____

_____

Expertise Area II:

_____

_____

_____

_____

_____

Be Unique! Unlike other programs, the *Social Designs* study abroad experiences includes parents in the preparation process and students in the development of their own learning objectives. It was a requirement for the facilitation team to be vibrant experts with the ability to challenge power structures, such as age ageism. Compared to other study abroad programs, Change Institute is very affordable.

How will your idea stand out from others?

_____

_____

_____

_____

_____

_____

Living out loud means trying new things. It is important to take calculated risks and sometimes sacrifice being "normal". When experiencing interruptions of living out loud, fight for your goals, have faith, and don't be afraid to stand out. There is nothing more powerful than knowing exactly who you are and refusing to apologize for your excellence. Don't be afraid to **live out loud, unapologetically.**

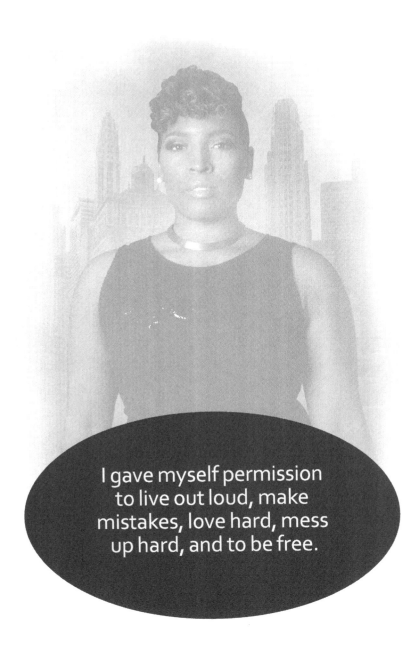

I gave myself permission to live out loud, make mistakes, love hard, mess up hard, and to be free.

4

INSPIRE YOURSELF

During my sophomore year of college, my father lost a long and tough battle with cancer. Along with my family and his close friends, I had to watch the process of him getting better and relapsing over and over again. It was the worse three years of my life. I lost my best friend, my motivator, my confidant, my provider, my pusher, and my rock. Life for me felt worthless without my Daddy. I did not want to eat, sleep, or go to class. I felt like there was nothing to push for if I wasn't doing it to make my Daddy proud. Luckily, I had a village of people to motivate and console me during hard times. I remember call my mom telling her I wanted to quit school. Her exact words were, "There will be no conversations nor negotiations about school, you will finish." My best friends went to neighboring universities, my sister was in the same city, and one of my favorite cousins always made sure I was better than just ok.

After a few months, I had to motivate myself to keep living and to keep striving for excellence. I knew that my support system would always be supportive, but they had lives too. I also knew that I needed to do well in school, so that I would be able to fully support myself and help my family, if needed, with the absence of my Daddy. I kept myself busy and involved in positivity. Having a full schedule was my way to keep my mind off of the pain. Although helpful in the short-term, I avoided the mourning process by keeping a packed schedule. Sadness and depression can creep in, settle, and produce a defeatist attitude, if you let it. I learned how to be ok with pain and discover new ways of healing; like being ok with crying, professional therapy, prayer, meditation, and allowing myself to appreciate life. This experience taught me the power of community and faith. After going through the turbulence of my dad passing, I was more mentally tough and able to utilize time in a more meaningful way.

As soon as I received my diploma, I was making a plan to be an entrepreneur and a philanthropist. In the meantime, of course I needed to work to pay bills, but that didn't mean I was not hungry for more and for better. In 2008, *Social Designs: by Jada* was created as a small business and it has blossomed in the last 8 years. There have been many renditions along the way and bumps in the road to success, but life is all about trial and error. I see errors or mistakes as **1- the opportunity to learn,** and **2- a reminder that I am human.** As Thomas Edison said, "I have not failed. I just found 10,000 ways that won't work."

After trial and error, losing money, dedicating millions

of hours of research, and sleepless nights; I'm a professional diversity and social justice consultant and trainer. This means I am implementing diversity and inclusion strategies, training staff in diversity and antiracist practices, and ensuring the retention of marginalized populations. As the CEO of *Social Designs,* a social justice consulting firm I manage 4 staff, design curriculums for clients, facilitate culturally competent workshops, train leaders, and create and implement study abroad programs for youth.

While leading an organization, I also strive to be involved so I can soak up as much information as possible. I want to be in the know and serve as a resource for my community. To stay in tune to with the millennial generation, I teach a course on Community Problem Solving at a small liberal arts college. This course helps students to develop a power and anti-oppression analysis for social change, while also serving in the community as service leaders and change agents. The course helps me understand this generation and how they feel about the world and social problems.

I volunteer on two boards; the American Friends Service Committee and ArtsGreensboro, and serve as a co-chair volunteer with the Greensboro Chamber of Commerce Other Voices Program. This work is critical. My involvement allows a few things, 1- **access to power** that I can leverage for marginalized communities, 2- **a learning opportunity** to grow my expertise in the diversity field, 3- **a place to use and refine my talents** so I can be a better professional, and 4- **an opening to connect people from various backgrounds** who wouldn't typically collaborate.

What organizations, programs, or initiatives can you connect with in order to be a more effective change agent?

_____

_____

_____

_____

In my 24 hours each day, I'd say that I'm pretty successful. I'm also tired. When I feel worn-out, I don't allow it to get in the way of my long term-goals. I seek out self-help books, articles, and webinars. Most importantly, I surround myself with positive people who push me to be a better person and more successful entrepreneur. These are all a few ideas that you can use to inspire yourself.

When I need a break or inspiration I visit art galleries, attend poetry slams, and spend time outside exploring nature. Every 3 -6 months I create a fresh vision board and hang it somewhere in my home where I can see it daily.

How are you inspiring yourself?

_____

_____

_____

_____

My inner circle keeps me vibrant and laughing. We travel, have family dinners, and have fun together.

Who around you is inspiring you and how are they inspiring you? List people you know personally.

_____

_____

_____

_____

Some people are just not good for you to be around. Whether they ignite bad habits or drain energy from you, they need to receive minimum energy from you.

Who around you is getting in the way of your success and how? List people you know personally?

_____

_____

_____

_____

I make it a habit to read *Teaching for Change* tips once a week and to watch a Marie Forleo webinar every two weeks to sharpen my teaching and professional skills.

Research & list 4-8 resources that will help you to refine yourself?

_____

_____

_____

_____

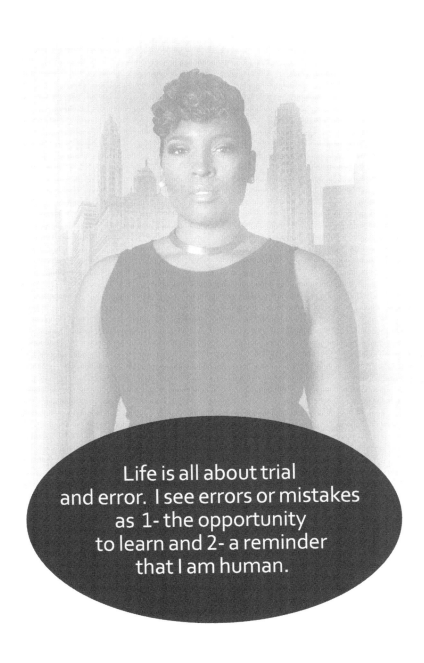

Life is all about trial
and error. I see errors or mistakes
as 1- the opportunity
to learn and 2- a reminder
that I am human.

5

BALANCE IS KEY

You will burn out and be ineffective in social change work if you do not find personal balance. Whether you are working within an organization or between multiple community groups, you must take time for you. Let me say it one more time, **YOU MUST TAKE TIME FOR YOU.** This sounds like an easy task, but as a person who enjoys helping people and working in this field, taking time for me used to be hard to do. It always seemed like the to-do list was never complete. I found myself in the rat race of life and work. I worked (and still do sometimes) very long hours and rarely took enough time to invest in myself.

Transparently, much of the rat race was self-induced as I was determined to earn a second degree with an ambitious goal to create and continue radical initiatives within the organizations I was a part of. After burning out, induced anxiety, unhealthy eating habits, and exhaustion, I think I found my healthy personal balance. It took me about seven years to get it right. I noticed that I became more effective, productive, and happy when I started following these three steps.

1. Meditating
2. Celebrating myself
3. Saying no

THE POWER OF MEDITATION

In the process of finally making the decision to fully pursue entrepreneurship, I begin to pray and meditate more. Meditation centers me in a spirit of gratitude. My mind is clearer and I am mentally prepared to face the challenges of the day. Russell Simmons, an advocate of meditation and balance, asserts, "I don't do shit until I meditate." This is my new mantra and it has proved effective. I do not leave the house without praying, meditating, and completing a 10 minute yoga routine. I encourage you to begin a meditation routine if you have not already started one.

When is the best time of the day for you to meditate? Are you an early riser? Do you set aside time in the evenings for you?

_____

_____

Realistically, how much time can you dedicate to meditation? Think about your schedule and then set an appointment with yourself. Sometimes I only have 5 minutes, but that 5 minutes makes a huge difference for me.

_____

_____

What do you need to focus? I need to have calming music with no lyrics (the Calm Meditation Pandora Station is a hit!) and low lighting. I also need a space in my house with no clutter in order to focus. What do you need to focus?

_____

_____

CELEBRATING MYSELF

What is the point of living life and not celebrating it? What fun is there in work, work, work and no play? Everybody needs to find a way to celebrate themselves as best they can. You must invest in yourself. One thing I always admired about my mom is that her nails were always bright red and pretty. She manicures and paints them every week. I absolutely hate painting my own nails, but I love the way my nails look when they are done. About 3 years ago, I started getting gel nail polish on my nails every 3 weeks. I love the smooth and finished look. I feel like a million bucks afterwards. But it's not just the after feeling for me. The salon I visit, Marianne's Brows, is very relaxing with soft music, low lighting, and elegant décor. Marianne and her staff are super nice and we always have great girl-talk and wine. For a small investment per month and about 40 minutes of my time I am rejuvenated.

I also invest in experiences that make me happy. Every quarter I budget for traveling. I enjoy learning and experiencing new countries and learning about unique cultures. I also attend as many live concerts as possible. I love live music! My mom is my ace when it comes to concerts because we love to dance and 'cut-up' together. Many social justice activist and revolutionaries do not celebrate themselves enough.

How can you celebrate yourself? What is it that makes you happy? Name three material things that make you happy and why. Then name three types of experiences that make you happy and why. Next, make it happen!

_____

_____

_____

_____

_____

_____

_____

_____

JUST SAY NO

If you are good at what you do, people will seek you out. As a young person in the field of diversity, I am asked constantly to be a part of this initiative, that board, or this program. As much as I want to help and add my expertise, I will not say yes to everything. After burning out from saying yes to too many things, I now have a few questions I work through before deciding to say yes, no, or later.

1. Do I have the time?

An old saying says that people make time for what they want to make time. This question is more like "Is this opportunity worth me shifting what is already in my schedule?" List out all of your obligations. How much time per week is each obligation? Take inventory of where your time is going. It is good to get a sense of your day to day, so when you are asked to do something new, you will be ready to respond.

_____

_____

_____

_____

_____

_____

_____

2. How is this going to benefit my professional growth and career?

Each time I add something to my schedule, I know exactly how it is going to benefit me in the long run. If I'm not growing, I'm not sowing. If it does not fit my purpose, it is not for me. It's simple. Monetary benefit is always nice, but that is not always the only benefit. For instance, I may have the opportunity to increase my influence or to gain more professional training. As a business owner, I may be able to gain more clients. Prepare yourself to say yes, or no. What are your growth areas? What career path or paths or you pursuing? What is your initiative or movement about?

_____

_____

_____

_____

_____

_____

_____

_____

_____

_____

_____

3. Why me?

In the last 5 years, I have made a name for myself nationally and internationally in the field of social justice particularly in higher education and non-profits. While growing my career, I have been asked to join quite a few boards. There are usually 3 reasons for the ask; 1) I'm bad-ass at what I do and I can bring a high level of expertise to the organization 2) I am usually considered to fulfill a diversity initiative in age, race, socio economic status, gender, etc. and 3) I am seemingly able to conform or assimilate to the culture of the organization or group.

You have to be careful and ask all of the right questions so you will know how to maneuver, get work done, and challenge the status quo. You also have to be careful not to pose and act as a token. A token is considered to be a person who is from an underrepresented group who is given access to power for the purpose of integration and equity or giving the appearance of equity within an organization or campaign. Be mindful that there are others that you can either suggest in place of you or groom to join or take your place. Cultivate leaders on the rise and spend time with them. Here are a few questions to ask yourself and the organization to access why they are interested in you and your expertise.

Why me? What do you anticipate me adding to this organization? Why did you not offer this opportunity to others? What was the criteria?

_____

_____

_____

_____

_____

_____

_____

_____

_____

How has the organization demonstrated action for social change?

_____

_____

_____

_____

_____

_____

_____

_____

_____

TOOLS
FOR ACTION
& SOCIAL
CHANGE

You will burn out and be ineffective in social change work if you do not find personal balance.

6

BUILD COMMUNITY

I'm from rural North Carolina and one of our staple dishes is macaroni and cheese. Macaroni and cheese fills the soul. Mac and cheese makes you feel good inside. The thing that I love about coming together during the holidays or for Sunday dinner is getting together to make macaroni and cheese with my family. The ingredients; eggs, milk, cheese (all kinds), mac shells, butter, oregano, peeper, salt, sour cream, and heavy whipping cream. Mac and cheese is made up of so many separate yet important ingredients and when they all come together, it is delicious! All of it melts together and when that happens, it looks a mess. Building community and organizing can look messy sometimes- it is not always easy to get the right mixture of people, events, and context to engage in organizing and building community. However, it is worth it in the end because when we bring people together we can make something that soothes our soul like that mac and cheese and it will provide us with the right nutrients to fight for justice.

When I think about revolution and people coming together I think about mac and cheese. One reason why is because it's a dish that traditionally brings us together. Secondly, mac and cheese is the essence of different ingredients coming together. When revolutionizing, it is important for people to work together. And not just work together in the way that we text, tweet, or post on Facebook; but true organizing that includes building friendships and building relationships.

Building strong and healthy communities should be our aim. A strong and healthy community is one that nourishes. It provides access to life enriching and life enhancing opportunities. It feeds the soul. It brings everyone to the table. Building a strong and healthy community is one that heals, restores, and tends to those who are most impacted and lack social support structures.

This chapter speaks to how to build community by **organizing, collaborating,** and building **sustainable relationships.**

ORGANIZING

When building community, organization is key! Organizing logistically as well as organizing people. The word organize used in different movements in various ways. I am defining organizing as **bringing people together to strategize around a common mission.** The way organizing happens is by honoring and acknowledging differences of opinions as well as being aware of social status. Responsible organizing also includes an assessment of your target audience. Are your asking elders to come to a meeting? If so, you may need to provide transportation. Are you organizing young adults? If so, do they need childcare?

Being in community and building community are two principles that are essential for organizing with a social justice lens. One of the beautiful things about organizing is that you get to bring people together. Organizing with an eye toward social justice encourages us to think deeply about the context of people's lives and to remove as many barriers of them being able to participate in the organizing process. Think about what might be some barriers for historically marginalized communities and how might they be addressed? Organizing for social justice invites us to engage the community to meet their needs. Knowing what matters to the community and providing them with the resources necessary to address the things that matter most to them is critical for organizing with a lens of social justice. It's never okay to drop into a community to promote your own agenda—it should always be about the people.

Some of the best organizing that I've witnessed is the El Roble community in El Salvador, Central America. As a faculty co-leader, I shared a social justice and community service experience with about 27 US students. The hosting organization CoCoDA (Companion Community Development Alternatives) created the opportunity for us to learn about the civil war in El Salvador, while also contributing to the rebuilding of the community school. The way our new friends in the community built relationship with us was genuine, slow, and intentional. I spent a lot of one on one time with the youth, elders, and young women to gain a perspective of the country and their daily life. The official language in El Salvador is Spanish. I speak very little Spanish so there was a language barrier, but tried not to let language be a barrier in getting to know people, by incorporating laughter, lots of body movements, and the help of others. CoCoDA did a great job setting up spaces for this type of interaction. We stayed with our host. We worked in small groups in the field, the kitchen, and at the school. We also played soccer, learned about history, danced, and celebrated life together.

I did not notice a spoken hierarchy of decision making in the community. People gave input from the perspective of their experiences and expertise, not strictly on their credentials. They also did a wonderful job training and learning from the young adult leaders. I was inspired by the careful and intentional intergenerational leadership.

Good organizers know that in order to bring people together, you have to give people what they want. Humans thrive off of feeling needed and like to be appreciated. Follow these four steps for effective organizing.

1. Make time for 1 on 1s
2. Follow Up
3. Celebrate
4. Create an Influence List

1 ON 1's

Take the time to get to know people on a one-on-one basis. Chart out great local restaurants or coffee shops where you can meet with people you seek to build community with.

Make it a habit to call people more often than texting. With an extremely hectic and jam packed schedule, it is hard for me to have as many one on ones as I would like to. However, I make it a point to connect with people on a personal basis as much as possible. One way of doing this is supporting others in their passion. Two of my best friends are coaches. I know I cannot make every single game to show my support, but each year I make it a point to make at least one game. If I cannot get to a game I show my support with a good luck call, supportive tweet, or Facebook shout out.

One on ones are also helpful when there is tension or conflict. I can remember many times as a college student, while working to create more equality on our campus, when my philosophy of change was completely different from a peer. Instead of 'knock out drag outs' in big groups, I began to meet with people individually with the purpose of seeking to understand their perspectives, share my experiences, and ultimately, discover how to work together.

Who do you need to sit down with in your community or organization to have a 1 on 1 with? What do you want to accomplish with your time with them? Where can you meet that supports local business?

_____

_____

_____

_____

_____

FOLLOW UP- REMINDERS

Be sure to send people reminders about community meetings, events, and campaigns. When you are organizing people with busy schedules, make sure you remind people of the importance of having their voice present. Also hold people accountable to attend the event. When I receive those email or calendar pop-ups to remind me of an event, it helps me tremendously. It may seem annoying or excessive, but if you want caliber, offer high caliber communication. One month, one week, three days, and same day reminders are typical within organizations.

What modes of communication reminders does your community respond to the most? What are communication limitations?

_____

_____

_____

_____

_____

_____

_____

_____

CELEBRATE

Are you celebrated life with your organizing team? Celebrate each victories and each other. Make sure you also around people who celebrate and appreciate you. A few winters ago, a group of well-respected young activists in Greensboro, NC organized a snowball fight when the city was shut down from a winter storm. They used this downtime as time to celebrate life and simply get together to build relationships. I find joy in celebrating people in multiple ways. I host dinners at my house and send encouraging texts messages. When I cannot make events, I make sure I send well wishes or a small gift to show gratitude.

How can you celebrate the people around you better?

_____

_____

_____

_____

_____

_____

_____

_____

_____

_____

CREATE AN INFLUENCE LIST

If you are looking to create long-lasting social change in an organization or community, knowing who the people of influence are is very important. Write down names of people you know in various systems. Then note the people who you need to know. Next cross-reference your list with people on your team. Lastly, create a strategy to get to know all of these people on a personal level so you can be more equipped to have a larger level of influence.

_____

_____

_____

_____

_____

_____

_____

_____

_____

_____

_____

SUSTAINBALE RELATIONSHIPS

Build relationships in an authentic way. Network in an authentic way. When you step into a room with new people, do not start going around just passing out business cards. Do not lead with your first question being, "What do you do?" Lead with getting to know someone. For example, "What is your name? What brings you here? What is your passion? How did you get to this place in your life? What do you like do? Tell me more about the city. Who do you know here and how?" Lead conversations with questions that take you and the other person on a storytelling journey. You will begin to understand the essence of each human. Oftentimes we talk about what we do and our credentials. None of those things matter if I do not know your passion and what drives you. When leading with these types of questions, you have the opportunity to share your passion and the reasons for wanting to create social change. In turn, the two of you are sharing energy and creating a synergy that is needed to revolutionize and to movement build.

During the civil rights movement, people came together. They marched together. They protested. This is true. However, prior to what is seen in the news clips and photos, people were creating those relationships. There were differing opinions. There were conversations that involved conflict. Yet they were able to work together more efficiently and more effectively because of strong relationships.

What are three questions you can ask people to get to know them on a deeper level?

_____

_____

_____

_____

_____

_____

What are three things you can openly share that will help
people understand you better?

_____

_____

_____

_____

_____

COLLABORATION

Collaboration sounds great and so lovely. Collaboration is
something that many people seek out whether it is in funding,
people power, marketing, or in creating awareness. Collaboration is awesome. Collaboration is also hard as hell. There
is a certain set of skills that are needed for effective collaboration. The first skill is **listening intently.** To listen intently,
you are stepping into a place where you are hearing the other
person's perspective and listening to a different opinion void
of your own, and you are challenging yourself to think differently. I have been in various cross-cultural environments
where the way I communicate or the words that I use, do
not mean the same as the person that is hearing me say the

words, resulting in a communication conflict. When you listen intently, you can create a space where you step back and you allow yourself to be misunderstood and misheard and are comfortable in that space.

The next step in advancing to another level of communication and intentional listening is **mastering patience.** You must be patient in repeating yourself and OK with over explaining. You will need to offer different words and different way of expressing yourself. You will even have to explore different tones in the way that you speak. All of these things are important when you step into a space to collaborate.

Collaboration also breeds creativity. Think outside the box. Actually, do not think that there is a box. When you step into a place of collaboration, bring all of your good energy and good vibes. Bring all of your awesome ideas. Bring your expertise and skill with you and share accordingly.

What are your creative powers?

_____

_____

_____

_____

_____

_____

_____

_____

What are your areas of expertise?

_____

_____

_____

_____

_____

_____

_____

_____

_____

INTENTION & EXPECTATION

When you are collaborating, intention and expectation must be explained thoroughly over and over again. What do you expect your co-collaborator to bring to the table? What timeline do you have in mind for success? What do you expect to get at the end of the project? How will you check in with each other on a regular basis? What do you expect of yourself? What do you expect of others? These questions are key to making sure that everyone involved has a clear understanding. Too many times, I have stepped into a collaboration without clear intentions or expectations and the road to our goals proved rocky until we cleared our expectations and intentions up more and more.

Use this chart the next time you collaborate.

Intentions & Expectations	You	Partner
Goals & Outcomes		
Timeline		
Specific Expectations		
Creative Powers		
Areas of Expertise		
Collective Goals		

Lead conversations with
questions that take you and
the other person or persons
onto a storytelling journey.

7

CALL A SPADE A SPADE

Injustice exists in communities around the world. This is a fact. We see people being discriminated against. We ourselves are often victims of injustice. Furthermore, we are often the culprit. What keeps vicious cycles of injustice going? Not calling the "it" out in the moment, after the moment, or after-after the moment. We also allow silence to get in the way of progress. Can you remember when you were called a bad name directly? Can you recall a time when you were referred to as something you are not, or by a condescending term? Have you ever been in a situation when in comparison to your friend or colleague, you were overlooked? Better yet, have you experienced micro aggressions? All of these instances could make you feel disrespected in some way or another.

When this happens, simply Call a Spade a Spade, communicate the obvious. Too often we try to 'sugarcoat' moments of conflict to sound nice or polite, when what we need to do is call a spade a spade. Do not call disrespect a mistake. Do not allow a condescending tone or comment to just fly by. Lasso 'that thing' out of the air and bring it to the ground. So many times I have seen people just let things that offend them go. The reason may be for safety, or fear, or even an inability to understand how to enter into deep conversation. Whatever the reason, we must have the courage to speak up. The way I choose to speak up may be different from how you speak up. We all have our comfort zones and our unique set of skills. However, we must begin to revolutionize by stating our story, our perspective, and our truth to open the conversation. How can we move towards change if no one knows change needs to happen? How does a child understand that drawing on your brand new white leather coach is the wrong thing to do? You tell them. How did men learn that the absence of women in leadership and in making decisions was not the best interest of the community? Women told them. Now we (women) are bosses and world leaders, we vote, and we are powerful. There are tons of ways to develop the conversation after it starts. But we must start by speaking up. #CallASpadeASpade

STEPS TO SPEAKING UP

There is a method I use in calling attention to problems or issues. The steps are interchangeable, but the components are present in each conversation. In every instance, the tone, immediacy, and delivery vary depending on my relationship to the people in the space and the greater goal in calling attention to the matter.

1. **FEEL IT!** If I have an emotion or feeling about an issue at hand, I do not ignore it. Most times when we feel something inside, we ignore it, especially in the professional setting. If you feel something do not ignore it. Ask yourself, "Why am I having this reaction?"

2. **SENSE IT!** Make some sense of what you are feeling. Make an educated guess about the person's intentions. Did the person mean harm or if they are simply acting out of habit or ignorance? Regardless of the sense you make, still make it your business to speak up. Assessing the situation helps you to create a strategy for speaking up.

3. **UNDERSTAND IT!** Understand the culture of the space. Is this a place where speaking out of turn or off topic is appreciated or looked down upon? Is this a culture where people take turns to speak? Is this a culture where difference of opinion is truly appreciated and welcomed? Knowing these things helps you to code what you are saying so that it is received.

4. **PUSH IT!** In following steps 1-3 know that the person or the people listening may disagree and may not give a hot damn about what you are seeking to relay. Don't stop. Keep speaking up. But understand that your strategy will need to become more sophisticated and multifaceted. Do

not be afraid or weary in needing to shift. In life, I have learned to be flexible and strategic in order to get the job done.

During my tenure as the Multicultural Education Department Director at Guilford College, a small liberal arts college in North Carolina, I began to Call a Spade a Spade, but with boldness and diplomacy. (Read more about being Bold, Diplomatic, & Nice later in the book). There were plenty of conversations that led to heightened emotions. Many of which were when I believed that colleagues were acting on privilege and perpetuating institutional racism. It was not easy to share with trusted colleagues in a Quaker institution, that they were fostering a racist environment. Quakers are greatly recognized for their role in the Underground Railroad, serving as champions for justice, and overall as 'good, liberal people.' Before speaking out verbally or even in writing, I questioned myself; "Am I tripping? Am I hypersensitive to race issues as a Black woman? Did they mean it that way? Maybe they did not? Should I say anything? I do not want to mess up my professional relationships with accusations." While the fear and questioning set in, I knew that my reaction was not false and that I had to address the issues and not be silent. There was resistance to my truth-telling and observations. There was also tension in the workplace for a while. But what came out of the tension was a light bulb moment for my colleagues, a better understanding of my position, insight to their thought process, and a greater respect for each other. This was possible because I created an atmosphere of Calling a Spade a Spade by developing shared meaning, calling in experts, and affirming people.

CREATING AN ATMOSPHERE OF CALLING A SPADE A SPADE

SHARED MEANING

When tackling large systemic issues, there must be a shared understanding of how the problem or issue is being defined. For years, I worked with a group of scholars, students, and community members toward the purpose of dismantling racism within an organization. When the institution asked consultants to come in to diagnose the problem, they predicted that major changes would happen after a 15 to 20 year timeframe. This prediction was based in the reality that the majority of citizens and residents of the United States do not understand 1- the definition of racism 2-the root causes of racism and 3-the ways racism is perpetuated on a daily basis. To undo the problem, the first step was to educate the community on relevant terminology and critical race theory. Together, we had to create shared meaning and a shared language.. Creating shared meaning becomes a critical process to create an atmosphere of Calling a Spade a Spade. Here are some important steps to consider when creating shared meaning.

1. Bring diverse people together
2. Create space for open dialogue
3. Invite folks to speak their truth
4. Listen, listen, and listen some more
5. Grapple & Synthesize
6. Take Action

CALL IN AN EXPERT

Great leaders understand the power of knowing when they do not know. They have the wisdom to call in experts when they are not experts themselves. Reaching out to consultants or other businesses to build on an idea, program, campaign, or new initiative is what successful people do. When faced with the task of changing a system, you must call in an expert to help you diagnose or assess the problem and a team of experts to assist in implementation. Additionally, as you embark on this new journey, you must also be willing to hire an expert to help you grow professionally.

I served as a consultant with a few organizations that wanted to change their organizations. Whether the change was to be more equitable or to create more efficiency within the team, what I repeatedly found is that the leader was not willing to first own up to their shortcomings. Most leaders saw that there was a problem or that the organization was facing a challenge. Many leaders failed to realize that their inadequacy was the major halt in progress. Calling a Spade a Spade is not only applicable when addressing a problem or issue. We must also look inward, call in an executive coach or connect with the human relations department to ask for professional development in the area that you as a leader might be lacking.

AFFIRM PEOPLE

A wise business consultant and women's empowerment coach once told me to lead a conversation that may seem controversial with two positives and you will be closer to your outcome. This tactic holds very true in all of the work I do. The strategy is one of sincerity and niceness; kind of like flirting, but in an appropriate professional way. When correcting a colleague, cancelling a meeting, or even declining a request, share two positives before offering the critical feedback or sharing disappointing news. For instance, "Hi, LaToya. I appreciate your hard work on this project and I value your expertise. From my perspective, a more engaging way to speak to elementary students is to literally get down on their level by sitting in a low chair or when talking." When you affirm people and offer solutions, you can get further in accomplishing your goal.

Do you have a challenge that you are seeking to solve? Have you hit a dead end in requesting to change a policy in your organization? Is there someone in the organization that just does not get it? Walk yourself through the steps below to get closer to your impact.

GUIDELINES

Use these guidelines to help guide you in calling a spade a spade in any situation.

Call a Spade a Spade. Determine what the problem or issue is at hand. What are you "calling out'" and why?

_____

_____

_____

_____

Affirm. Who are you working with to resolve the problem or get to the goal? Be sure to acknowledge their previous work or their contribution to the organization or cause. What has this person or group of people done already toward the cause?

_____

_____

_____

_____

_____

_____

Present the 'Ask'. Be 'tight' in how you present what it is you are seeking to change or revolutionize. Be clear, concise, and creative. What exactly are you asking for?

_____

_____

_____

_____

_____

_____

_____

Allow Space for Clarification. Understand that just because you make sense to you doesn't mean that you make sense to other people. Be open to people's sincere curiosity. Do not be defensive. As you answer questions, try to over explain. What are questions that you can anticipate?

_____

_____

_____

_____

_____

Give Examples. Be sure to have your data in hand when you are seeking to revolutionize. You want to make sure that your data (qualitative & quantitative) backs up your creative action idea. What are your tangible examples?

_____

_____

_____

_____

_____

_____

Invite an Expert. Search the field locally, regionally, nationally, and internationally to find a reputable expert who can back up your ideas for social change and who can speak to the issue. Look for a local expert who would be willing to share pro-bono or a reduced honorarium. If you cannot afford to have a national or international professional visit your organization, simply Skype them in for a quick conversation. Who are your experts?

_____

_____

_____

_____

_____

Follow Up. People are not going to solve your problem for you. Keep the conversation and strategy moving forward by checking in with people on a consistent basis. What is your follow up frequency?

_____

_____

_____

_____

_____

Bring Attention. After about 3 months, access your campaign, strategy, or creative action plan to gauge if there has been any progress. If there is no movement and if people are being complacent, bring media attention to your cause.

Begin to develop a relationship with the media now, so that the relationship will not be so transactional. What media contacts do you have? Who can you connect with for various causes? Be sure to include social media and blog contacts as well.

Truth propels us to understand each other from a deep level of spirit and humanity.

8

BE BOLD, DIPLOMATIC, & NICE

One of my formulas for successful partnerships and solutions in the field of social justice is being BOLD+ DIPLOMATIC + NICE. The combination of the three has allowed for success personally and professionally. In life you have to be bold to let the world know your courage and serious nature. You also need to be nice to work with people and sustain relationships. Diplomacy is the skill that I have worked the hardest on because it takes a lot of effort to be tactful in stressful situations.

BOLD

Bold: (of a person, action, or idea) showing an ability to take risks; confident and courageous.[8]

One thing I have not had a problem with is being bold. As a child I would often do outrageous things and always

(almost too much) share my opinion. I get a huge adrena-
line rush in taking risks. It's in my nature to be bold. All of
my friends know that if there is ever a dare on the table, I am
the one to take it on.

On a more professional level, in the field of diversity,
equity, and inclusion, there are times when being bold does
not come so easy. When faced with extreme conflict, I have
stood in shock, silence, disbelief, hurt, or anger. It is tough
to be bold, when you are trying to figure out how you feel
about a situation and have no clue how to react. However, I
believe that to stand up for what I believe is the most socially
conscious way. Acknowledgement is a first step to speaking
up. You may not have a strategy or fully understand the topic
at hand, but if you have the courage to ask questions, make
suggestions, or share your opinion, the conversation will shift.

DIPLOMATIC
. . . .
Diplomacy is showing an ability to deal
with people politely. Diplomacy is also
engaging tact when in stressful
situation.[5]
. . . .

I often ask myself, "How do I call a spade a spade in a diplomatic way? I mean seriously, how do I tell a VP, Department Head, Principal, or elder that their approach makes
absolutely no sense and if they move forward with it they will
lose all respect from their constituents? How do I tell a trusted
colleague that they are sexist to the point of no return?" You

can definitely say these things verbatim. You can be as blunt as you want. But what will come with that is defensiveness, anger, and avoidance. Think about it, if someone were telling you about yourself, 'reading you' or 'putting you in your place,' how would you react? You would be defensive, angry, and maybe even avoid the conversation. It is normal for these feelings to come up.

So if you want to get to a greater goal and are seeking to revolutionize, learn to be diplomatic. This skill will get you closer to your goal. When first being taught this skill, I was frustrated. I could not understand why my mentors were asking me to 'sugar coat' the truth. I didn't feel authentic or sincere if I wasn't letting people know my truth as I saw it. I had to remove Jada from the situation and remember the reason for the conversation, program or project. Now, I'm skilled in coupling being bold with being tactful, or diplomatic. It is less important for me to win and more important for me to get the team or group to the greater goal and vision.

NICE
Nice: kind, polite, and friendly[6]

As a social justice activist, it is a requirement for me to be nice. No one likes a scrooge. I account much of my success to just being an overall nice person. Think about one of the meanest teachers, family members, children in school growing up, or community members. I am sure that you never wanted to be in their presence, learn anything from them, or respect them. The same thing goes for doing social change work. If you are mean and grumpy all the time, people are going to be worn down. Can you call a spade a spade and be bold while being nice? Absolutely! Being nice does not mean shying away from truth. It just means that you are graceful, polite, and patient with people. When sharing your truth, sometimes you may hurt people's feelings. When pointing out inequities, discrimination, and acts of violence, sometimes people will be offended or challenged. However, we must be truthful and real at all times to see social change. And we can all do this in a nice way.

I get pissed off often when doing work to revolutionize systems and processes. The 'pisstivity' does not go away immediately and I have to talk through situations while my emotions and passion are heightened. It is draining work. It is heart work. Now, this is where being nice can be a bit hard to do. What I often do is state the obvious to allow time for me to cool down. For example, "The situation at hand and the comments that I'm hearing are very disturbing and I need a moment to respond appropriately and professionally." Sometimes, you just need to let people know, without letting them know, that you are upset or angry. I have found that this sets a tone for intentional listening and respect. No matter what, always stay professional, meaning I'm saying what I need to say in a way that gets my point across. Does this mean that I am not raising my voice or that I'm not communicating passion? Does this mean that I am meek and lowly?

Heck no! This means that no matter what, I'm in control of myself. I always keep the end goal in mind to ground me.

The topics I teach and train about like societal issues and inequities are emotional and heavy. It is ok to be emotional. As a facilitator, I invite all of my emotions into the space. Sometimes I cry, express anger, and communicate sadness. However, what I do not do is allow my emotions to take over the space.

I encourage you to bring your full authentic self when discussing and debating controversial issues. There is fine line between diplomacy and neutrality. Sometimes neutrality is helpful if you are moderating with the goal of flushing out a problem and uncovering solutions. As you move towards solutions, try not to be defensive and 'stay out of your feelings.' Do engage in your passion and bring your perspective with a spirit of urgency. **Be bold, diplomatic, and nice.**

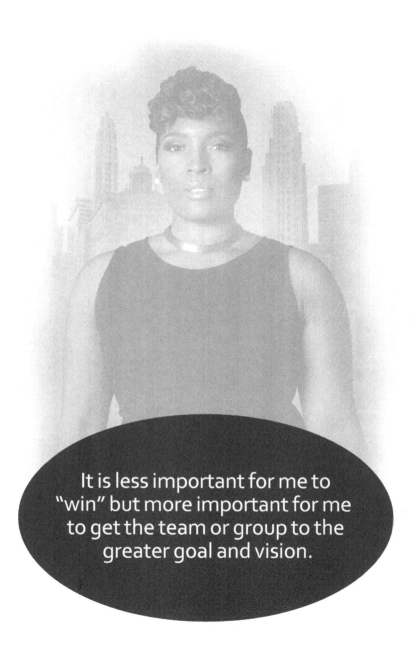

It is less important for me to "win" but more important for me to get the team or group to the greater goal and vision.

9

RESIST & REVOLT

In my experiences working within organizations, my skills of conflict resolution, communication, training and development, and strategic planning have been key to my success in being a part of creating action for collective social change. My perspective is often limited to organizational perspectives (non-profit, higher education, governmental), as that is where I have spent most of my time engaging this work. With that, it is important for me to connect with other social justice organizations and people who work directly on the ground. I have friends who are lawyers, teachers, business owners, politicians, police officers, youth leaders, clergy, corporate employees, coaches, etc. Being connected helps me to have varying perspectives that inform this work, especially when I am able to bring people together for a united cause. My revolutionary gifts are connecting people, training, and teaching. It's important to discover what your revolutionary gifts are as you embark on a journey of creating social change.

What are your revolutionary gifts? How can you utilize your
skills and talents to interrupt unhealthy systems?

_____

_____

_____

_____

_____

_____

_____

Here are direct action steps for you to engage resisting
and revolting.

PERSONAL POWER

Analyze
Own Up
Step Down
Vote
Study Revolutionaries

COLLECTIVE POWER

Document
Create
Demand & Expose

PERSONAL POWER

ANAYLZE

I'm passionate about increasing the economic sustainability and profitability of Black people. But before moving into solutions, it's important to understand the historic evidence of Black communities owning resources and holding political power. Ten years ago I began to research the development and the disenfranchisement of 'Black Wallstreets' in the United States of America. Historically, these communities suffered from systemic and governmental genocide, the implementation of highways destroying infrastructure, and institutional racism. Currently, many Black communities are negatively affected by issues of the past. Yet, there is also a need to analyze the personal power and engagement or lack thereof, of the people in these communities. You have to analyze the problem to understand it. Comprehension is key in uncovering solutions for social change. In exploring social justice and resistance, know as much about the subject matter before moving into solutions.

What perspectives are missing in your analysis of your social justice issue? Research your issue and ask for similar and opposing views to strengthen your understanding and approach.

_____

_____

_____

_____

_____

_____

_____

_____

_____

_____

_____

OWN UP

I'm a skilled professional in the social justice field and I mess up as a young revolutionary. For example, during a very heated time in Greensboro, North Carolina, I was asked to be one of the facilitators for a community dialogue the City of Greensboro organized in response to many protests and strategic meetings. These meetings were specifically facilitated by elders, such as activist Rev. Nelson Johnson, to address police brutality and accountability.

At the beginning of the packed forum, there was a collective of unsatisfied sentiment from some community members. There were comments expressing that the conversation was not initiated in unity with the community, but a political move by the city. We listened to the opinions and heard the demand for restructuring the conversation to include more community leaders as facilitators. A major concern was that none of the facilitators were Black men; who are of the most negatively affected populations in the city. I realized in that moment; "Oh shit, I'm a part of the problem. I have just been tokenized and did not make a responsible decision in agreeing to facilitate this forum." What I wish I had done was ask more questions, connect with more community members to learn the full backstory, and request Black male representation.

The people spoke, the organizers and community leaders collaborated, and the forum continued. Black males co-facilitated in our small groups. A trusted friend with whom I have built community with over the years, an activist, David "Irving" Allen and I paired up and had a valuable discussion with our group. During the forum, I was hype because of the collective community power. People stood up, spoke up, and demanded a more inclusive process for discussing social change.

Conversely, I was also disappointed in myself for not being reflective enough to take myself out of the rat race of a crazy schedule and reach out to others who had been organizing around this issue as soon as I was asked to facilitate. Instead, I assumed that there was some consultation with those who had been leading these conversations in the community, and agreed to facilitate.

Immediately after the forum, I shared this letter with Black male leaders:

March 23, 2015

Rev. Johnson, David, & TC,

Thank you all for your leadership tonight. I appreciate your persistence, intelligence, courage, strategy, and genuine support for the people. The shift in this conversation was a breath of fresh air.

In being asked to facilitate this conversation, I asked myself, "Is Beloved Community Center involved. I then talked to a member of BCC about what was the most important thing to bring into the conversation tonight. They shared their prospective, most of which I planned to bring into my small conversation.

I repeat, which "I" planned to bring into MY small conversation group.

After reading our prompt questions, I knew they were not deep enough. I thought I would do a good activist deed by making sure the concerns of the community were to be in the space. I planned to make those inserts where necessary.

The problem here is I didn't call either of you to ask, "Hey this is happening, I have this role, what should I do & how can this process be changed?

When I walked into the pre-training room today and saw that there were no facilitators from BCC or moreover no facilitators that were Black males I didn't make the point. I didn't make it an issue.

I'm sincerely upset with myself for not getting out of the "I" that I talk to my students about avoiding.

I apologize for not reaching out before. I apologize for being a hypocrite.

I look to continue to evaluate my role in the community and in education, and as a budding activist.

In love,
Jada

I share this story because it is an example of how to be transparent as a revolutionary. You may not always get everything right, but you must own up to your mistakes. The responses I received from my message were all affirming. One of which was from my good friend and revolutionary, Terence "TC" Muhammad saying: "Girl please. No need to apologize to us. You're no hypocrite. We all need sharpening and reminders. NONE of us are perfect. You are family."

What is it that you need to own up to in your social justice work? Maybe it is just acknowledging here in the notes or you can make a point to reach out to the people you have built community with to share your reflections.

_____

_____

_____

_____

_____

_____

STEP DOWN

There are people in social change work who need to step down because 1- they do not know what they are doing or 2- it is time to allow new voices to step up. If you are leading an effort and you do not have the proper expertise, step down from the leadership role. Remember the movement is not about you, it's about progress and social change. In my role with the National Youth Action Project of the White Privilege Conference, I am the co-leader of creating a transformative experience for 500+ youth each year. This means I am in charge of everything. However, certain aspects of the job require leadership from others. As much as I enjoy being a key decision maker, it feels so much better to step down and allow the team to take control of the parts where their expertise is best.

Our elders in social justice need to consider how they are passing the torch to the next generation. We need a transfer of power, knowledge and skill. Holding on to power stunts the progression of communities. Some elders are really good at grooming the next generation. Some, however, are making a life in fighting for struggle instead of supporting youth in discovering solutions to end the struggle.

Name a time in the past or a current project where you know that you needed to let go and step down. What do you need to do next to make sure the project or organization does not suffer?

_____

_____

_____

_____

_____

_____

VOTE

Make your voice count by voting for your city, county, state, and national candidates. Research the candidates and organize around a candidate that you and your constituents can hold accountable to your needs.

Who are your city, county, state, and national officials? Who is running for the next election? Be in the know. Be civically engaged.

_____

_____

_____

_____

_____

_____

_____

_____

STUDY REVOLUTIONARIES

There is no need to reinvent the wheel. Research and study people who have shared their creative leadership with the world. Learn from and lean on revolutionaries who have initiated and sustained social change. Here are examples of great revolutionaries to know and study. Examine those in your community to gain a clear sense of how you can move forward in your social change strategy.

INTERNATIONAL REVOLUTIONARIES

1. Fela Anikulapo Kuti
2. Bob Marley
3. Chimimanda Ngozi Adiche
4. Kendrick Lamar
5. Tupac Shakur
6. Nelson Mandela
7. Mother Teresa
8. Rev. Nelson & Joyce Johnson
9. Bishop Oscar Romero
10. Bayard Rustin
11. Audrey Lorde
12. Assata Shakur
13. The Black Panther Party
14. Queen Nanny
15. Oscar Micheaux
16. Rev. Dr. Martin Luther King, Jr.
17. Mahatma Gandhi
18. Dolores Huerta
19. Malcolm X
20. Che Guevara
21. Fidel Castro
22. Ruby Dee Davis
23. Bussa (Barbados)
24. Mandy Carter
25. Zora Neale Hurston
26. Steve Biko
27. Berta Caceres
28. Malala Yousafzai
29. François-Dominique Toussaint Louverture
30. Pauli Murray
31. Christopher Everett
32. Paulo Freire
33. Aiko Herzig-Yoshinga
34. Harvey Milk
35. Desmond Tutu
36. Nettie Coad
37. Nat Turner
38. Nowa Cumig, Dennis Banks
39. Zumbi dos Palmares
40. C. Odumegwu Ojukwu
41. _____
42. _____
43. _____
44. _____
45. _____

COLLECTIVE POWER

DOCUMENT

Documentation and evidence speaks volumes. Document stories and incidences administratively and create a place for unsolicited data to help inform action. There is power in story-telling and personal accounts. Some people move to action and social change through data and information. Some are moved by individual and collective stories. Much of my liberation started as I explored authors like Audrey Lorde and Paulo Freire to name a couple. My own story also empowered me.

What types of data collection and data analysis systems are in place to help you analyze inequity in your organization? If none exist, what can you implement? How can you document and share your own experiences as a teaching tool?

_____

_____

_____

_____

_____

_____

Who are authors you can lean on for a better understanding of social change? What is it about your story that will help

someone understand your perspective or that will ignite social change?

_____

_____

_____

_____

_____

_____

_____

CREATE

Create a new standard if the current organization is not working. The Black Panther Party for Self Defense is a great example of creating demands for social systems, while also creating programs to uplift and empower community. (See appendix for the Black Panther Party10 Point Program.) The party initiated programs focused on education, nutrition, health, the arts, and clothing for the community. In 1972, the American Indian Movement organizers of Minneapolis created, Survival Schools as a strategy to combat high drop-out rates. The focus areas were Indian culture and basic living and learning skills.1 Oscar Micheaux, Stephen Hayes, and Cynthia Lockhart create works of art to ignite social change. Visual artists, musicians, filmmakers, writers, poets, and fashion designers all play a part in providing an alternative method of understanding how social change can happen in a creative way.

What innovative idea do you have? What can we do that challenges the status quo and creates social change?

_____

_____

_____

_____

_____

DEMAND & EXPOSE

Thousands of college students are holding their school's administration accountable by resisting oppressive policies on campus. They publicize demands because they understand the severity of inequity, bias, and unfair treatment. Develop and share your demands widely with all leaders and constituencies of the organization. Don't be afraid to alert local, state, and national news too. (See Appendix for an example of demands.) What are your demands? What is your accountability schedule and strategy for holding organizations accountable to the demands?

Demands	Accountability Deadlines	Strategy

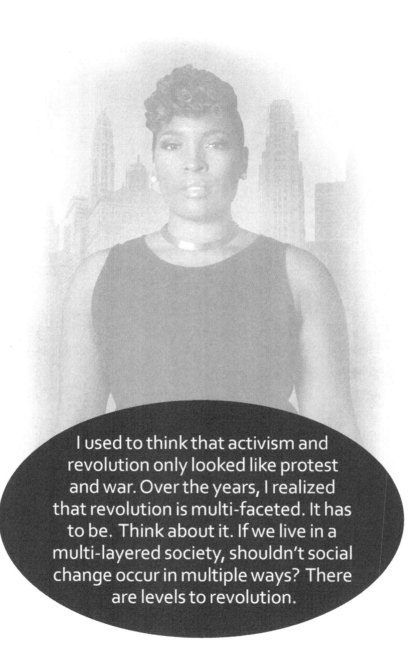

I used to think that activism and revolution only looked like protest and war. Over the years, I realized that revolution is multi-faceted. It has to be. Think about it. If we live in a multi-layered society, shouldn't social change occur in multiple ways? There are levels to revolution.

10

DO IT NOW!

It is painful to be part of organizations that have a mission for justice, yet the actions of the people counteract the actualization of the mission. I lead a lot of departmental, board, and community meetings that are extremely torn and frustrated because of the lack of clarity, vision, expertise, and strategy to implement strong and radical policy that will have lasting effects in the organization and the community. Social change workers often go wrong when getting too wrapped up in feelings and emotions. It can get to a point of stunting the ultimate growth of an organization. For example, in my work with a few national non-profit groups, I am often frustrated with two things; 1- Not charting the impact of equity and inclusion work in a cost benefit analysis and 2- Reluctance in seeing the benefit of further developing skills in management, communication, and conflict resolution across lines of difference such as class, gender identity, philosophy, or race.

Most unresolved or intensified conflict is due to a lack of training. Some people get a pass for not being excellent in what they do. I say ... **Do better, try harder, be excellent, or get out of the way.** If you are going to invest in social justice work, you must invest in and understand the power of professional development.

When you are organized, have found your team, built with your community, analyzed the issue, and have worked to discover your power and privilege, **REVOLUTIONIZE.** There is no time like the present. Don't let anyone let you think that your issue, your pain, or your liberation is not immediate. Revolutionize with a spirit of urgency. What will happen if you wait? Who will suffer? Who will benefit? I am writing this book from a place of heteronormative, economic, formal education, and Christian privilege. There have been times when my actions are not immediate enough due to blind spots. There have been times when I'm not 'woke' enough. I try to surround myself with people who will challenge me in my areas of privilege as much as possible. I know from being challenged that my blind spots are often caused by gender and religious privilege.

Discover Your Blind Spots
Where are your blind spots? What is the root cause of your blind spots? Figure out your growth areas and seek to change.

_____

_____

_____

_____

_____

There are multiple forums to make social change happen. Large meetings or forums allow for multiple voices and different perspectives. This is a great place to call people or groups to action and support accountability. Some leaders tend to get defensive in open forums, therefore you may need to set up small group or individual meetings to get closer to your goal. Before setting anything up, make sure your team or constituents know what will be discussed and follow-up with the group. This is a method that successful business leaders use too. Important decisions can occur over a drink, dinner, or a more personable setting. Why is this? There are multiple reasons. Some people make hard decisions when they are more comfortable. Some people need to be persuaded differently. Assess your situation, plan accordingly, and take action.

Revolutionizing creatively is the key. What are you doing differently? Are you offering new solutions or are you only offering up a synopsis of the problem? While developing your action, be sure to have key players ready to work. I believe it is important to have multiple methods and different types of people leading revolution. There are The Protestors, The Public Speaker, The People, The Persuaders, The Power Brokers. The key is connecting everyone for collective impact. Which type of revolutionary are you? Do you know and work with other types of revolutionaries? Why or why not? How?

"ROLE" CALL - WHO'S IN YOUR SQUAD?

The Protestors – The activists who always organize and show up with a purpose to support or oppose a view. Protestors take many forms. There are silent protestors. There are protestors who call attention to issues by showing up and shutting down the normative way of systems. Name a few in your organization or community.

_____

_____

_____

The Public Speaker – They are the ones who can motivate groups of people to action. They are fully aware of their audience and can grab the attention of various stakeholders. Name a few in your organization or community.

_____

_____

_____

The People – Those you can call on to show up. They show up because they believe in the organizers and the cause. They understand that there is power in numbers. The People are also called on to do specific things within various industries. Know the talent pool of the people; cooks, artists, accountants, etc. Name a few in your organization or community.

_____

_____

_____

The Persuaders – Persuaders are those who are within systems who have the charm, wit, and strategy to influence people to shift thinking, direct resources, or make bold organizational statements or initiatives that will influence masses of people and leaders in power. Name a few in your organization or community.

_____

_____

_____

The Power Brokers – These are people who have the power to make big and quick decisions in your organization or community. This power may be in influence or capital. Name a few in your organization or community.

_____

_____

_____

Once you have identified your squad, take action.

DO IT NOW!

Take Control – The push for social change by student leaders across the nation in 2015 is the perfect example of having powerful, revolutionary, and strategic teams. Locally, many of the students whom I had the honor to groom, organized their community, built a squad, and held their College community accountable. Take a look at the demands they presented to Guilford College in the appendix. They organized collectively with a "Squad" and transformed the demands into strategic accountability student club, *Integrity for Guilford* and a developing course on creative leadership for social change. You can take control of your issue too. Here are a few things to consider:

Develop Collective Demands – Work together with people who are interested in creating social change to present demands to the leaders of the organization. **What are the top three social justice issues in your organization or local community? List the issues and list the demands.** Then select one collective action or task that you can align on with others from the community for large collective impact that will have an effect on many issues at once.

	Root of problem	People most affected	Demands from a specific organization to address the problem	One collective action item that will address the problem of all three issues
Social Justice Issue 1 _____ _____ _____ _____				
Social Justice Issue 2 _____ _____ _____ _____				
Social Justice Issue 3 _____ _____ _____ _____				

Involve the National Organizations – The EEOC- The Equal Employment Opportunity Commission is an organization to connect with directly when you observe inequity and discrimination. There are other national organizations like Glass Door to report organizations and schools. **Who can you work with to 1- take legal action or 2- expose the inequity?**

_____

_____

_____

_____

Connect to the Top – Discover the leaders who are at the top. If there is a president, there are members of a board that manage the president. If there is a principal, there is a school board. Once you discover leaders, find a way to connect with those leaders. It may be requesting a meeting or sending an email. Just do it now. Do not wait. **Who do you need to connect with at the top?**

_____

_____

_____

_____

Create a doable and effective plan of action. You are not here to make the entire universe a better place. Create this plan with your team and constituents. Carve out a doable action plan for one issue or problem every nine months to a year before you add too much to your list of obligations. Understand your capacity and your resources (refer to Balance is Key) and then set a doable and effective plan of action. What is one issue or cause you can focus on for the next nine months? Set one, three, five, seven, & nine month goals. Stick to your goals dates, but be willing to be flexible.

Month One Goals

_____

_____

_____

_____

_____

Month Three Goals

_____

_____

_____

_____

_____

Month Five Goals

_____

_____

_____

_____

_____

Month Seven Goals

_____

_____

_____

_____

_____

Month Nine Goals

_____

_____

_____

_____

_____

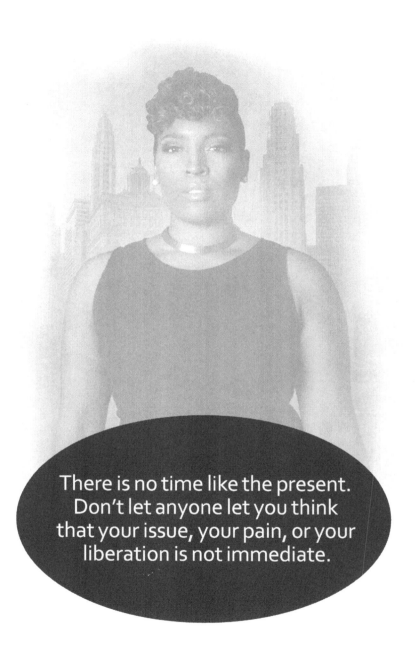

There is no time like the present. Don't let anyone let you think that your issue, your pain, or your liberation is not immediate.

11

CONCLUSION

I am no longer accepting the things I cannot change. I am changing the things I cannot accept.

— ANGELA DAVIS

It's 'time out' for mediocre action for social change. I am challenging myself to be even more creative in my leadership. What propelled me to write Revolutionize Now was aggravation with organizations. I would sit in multiple meetings and could not understand why systemic change took so long. It is true that societal shifts require assessment, strategy, and time. I get it. But in 2016 there should not be such a large disparity of wealth or a huge gap in education and health disparities along racial and gender lines. I challenge you to use self-reflection and the tools of this book to require more and to engage in collective action for social change.

Require more of yourself and of the people in the communities you serve. We have the power to re-shape or create whatever change we wish to see in the world. Yes, we need to hold leaders with "power" accountable to service the community. We also need to invest in our families and our communities while divesting from mental captivity, bad habits, and organizations that are not in our best interest.

I hope that you connect with other change agents around you to develop creative and collective action for social change. For example, focus on improving the unemployment rate by 2% by working with community members to create employment opportunities; work with local businesses when demanding equality from higher education institutions; or connect all the churches in a city to build Freedom Schools. Think outside the box and reframe your understanding of the word revolution. It starts with you and continues with all of us.

You have the power.
We have the power.
Revolutionize Now.

With radical love,
Jada Monica Drew

ΛCKNOWLEDGEMENTS

I am blessed beyond measure for the opportunity for God to use me to motivate others. I am grateful for the many experiences in life that have shaped me to be the woman I am today. I know that it is my purpose to build community and to connect people. Each day I am working to be more present, more intentional, and more inclusive in my thinking and actions.

Thank you to my family and friends for believing in me, for teaching me lessons, and celebrating life with me.

Thank you to all of the many students of Guilford College, Youth Action Project-White Privilege Conference, James B. Dudley High School, Willis Hare Elementary, and beyond! Special thank you to the Africana CHANGE Alumni and the 2016 Spring Justice& Policy Studies Community Problem Solving Class of Guilford College for your contributions to this book and to my life as a teacher and learner.

Thank you to the Greensboro Chamber of Commerce Other Voices Program for enhancing my analysis of equity and encouraging deep spiritual connections. Special thanks to Mary Kendrick, Lee Jeffers, Joyce Gorham-Worsley, Dar-Linda Finch, Addy Jeffery, & Yamile Nazar and OV Class 21

Thank you to James Shields and the Bonner Scholars Program for teaching me the foundations of social justice.

Thank you to the production team of Revolutionize Now:

Editors: Durryle Brooks, Bevelyn Afor Ukah, & Holly Wilson

Photographer: Curtis Smith of CSJ Photography

Book Design: KPE Media

JADA'S SOCIAL JUSTICE & EMPOWERMENT PLAYLIST

1. 99 Problems, Jay Z
2. Young, Gifted, & Black, Nina Simone
3. Man in the Mirror, Michael Jackson
4. Til it Happens to You, Lady Gaga
5. Be Alright, Kendrick Lamar
6. Redemption Song, Bob Marley
7. Blacker the Berry, Kendrick Lamar
8. King James, Jasiri X
9. What's Going On, Marvin Gaye
10. Fight the Power, Public Enemy
11. A Song for Assata, Common
12. All Black Everything, Lupe Fiasco
13. Drama, Erykah Badu
14. Waist Deep in the Big Muddy, Pete Seeger
15. Closer, Goapele
16. Get It Together – India Arie
17. Apple Tree – Erykah Badu
18. Buffalo Solider, Bob Marley
19. So Much Trouble, Bob Marley
20. Worth His Weight in Gold, Pulse

21. Rebel, Lee Scratch Penny

22. Farming, Rootz Underground

23. I Wanna Yell, Elan

24. We Gon Be Alright, Kendrick Lamar

25. You Can't Stop Us, Nas

26. Change Gone Come, Sam Cooke

27. Faithful, Common

28. I Find It Hard to Say (Rebel), Lauryn Hill

29. If I Ruled the World, Nas

30. Love Is Stronger Than Pride, Sade

31. Changes, Tupac

32. Glory, John Legend & Common

33. Ye Yo, Erykah Badu

34. Freedom Time (LIVE), Lauryn Hill

35. Love Yourz, J. Cole

∧PPENDIX

Black Panther Party Ten Point Program[10]

1. We want freedom. We want power to determine the destiny of our Black Community.

2. We want full employment for our people.

3. We want an end to the robbery by the white man of our Black community.

4. We want decent housing, fit for shelter of human beings.

5. We want education for our people that exposes the true nature of this decadent American society. We want education that teaches us our true history and our role in the present-day society.

6. We want all black men to be exempt from military service.

7. We want an immediate end to POLICE BRUTALITY and MURDER of black people.

8. We want freedom for all black men held in federal, state, county and city prisons and jails.

9. We want all black people when brought to trial to be tried in court by a jury of their peer group or people from their black communities, as defined by the Constitution of the United States.

10. We want land, bread, housing, education, clothing, justice, and peace.

Student Demands – Guilford College[2]

1. The creation and implementation of a publicly overseen diversity plan. We insist on a shift towards intentional and responsible representation of diversity in marketing, rather than the tokenizing of students of color in marketing material that exists now. Guilford is marketed as a safe space for students of color, but that is not the reality.

2. The hiring of more people of color in faculty, staff and resident advisor positions.

3. Students of color be treated with respect and dignity.

4. A proper breakdown and accountability process from our school's public safety.

5. College administrators, professors, and staff must publicly acknowledge their racism, be it overt, covert, or passive.

6. Full and clear accountability from Campus Life in relation to the judicial process.

7. Guilford College must embark upon a transparent strategy to increase retention rates for marginalized students, and sustain diversity curricula for all marginalized students.

8. Departments dedicated to the recruitment, retention and support of queer students, students of color, and international students must be sufficiently funded and staffed.

9. The creation of a sovereign Office of Diversity and Inclusion to enforce these demands and keep the administration accountable – these tasks should not solely be carried out through the unpaid labor of students and faculty of color.

SOCIAL DESIGNS ACTIVITIES AND TIPS FOR CREATIVE SOCIAL CHANGE

Lyric Me This – Artistic Engagement of Hard Topics

Choose a song that creates conversation around a social justice topic of choice. Ask participants to listen o the lyrics, tone, and mood of the song. Instruct them to create a visual representation of how they analyze the song and how the song makes them feel. Have them share pictures and share out. See Jada's Social Justice & Empowerment Playlist for song ideas.

Steps to Create Higher Education Organizational Shift

1. Implement a Climate Assessment

2. Research the History of Liberation & Oppression on Campus (Center funded or semester course)

3. Hire a Consultant

4. Development Equity & Inclusion Plan

5. Create a Funded Task Force with Accountability & Implementation Power

6. Transform the interior design and diverse representation in portraits and paintings

7. Include multiple modes of teaching for every discipline

8. Develop a training series for culturally responsive curriculum for all disciplines

9. Examine contractors, vendors, consultants to determine if pool is diverse

10. Create affinity alumni groups

11. Require series of equity analysis training for upper level leaders

12. Organize collective trips off campus to learn about the community.

Culture Wheel – Community Building Tool

The purpose of the activity is for participants to share their cultural practices with each other in an interactive and engaging manner.

Step One-

Split the group up in groups of 4-8. Participants do not need any paper or pencil/pen for this exercise. Have each group create their own standing circle facing inward.

Step Two-

Explain that we are about to play a game. This game is about sharing their individual culture with one another. Explain what each category means and give an example.

Step Three-

Hand each member one of the sheets of paper with a component and ask them to stand on it. Everyone needs to stand in a circle facing each other. Ask everyone to shift one component to the left.

Step Four-

Instruct participants to share their culture as it relates to the component they are standing on. Highly encourage participants to include as much detail as possible when sharing. After each person shares in the circle, everyone will rotate and share another component until everyone has shared from each component.

General Components:

Traditions
Words/Phrases
Nicknames
Ethnicity (ies)
Food
Music
Home
Surroundings/Neighborhood
Race
First Language

Explanations & Examples of the Components

Traditions – Rituals, heritage events
   Ex-Blue light Basement, CIAA

Words – unique dialect, words, or language
   Ex- Fitna=about to

Phrases – a lesson or riddle
   Ex-The grass is always greener on the other side

Nicknames – another name referred to a person for a reason or not
   Ex-Jada Pooh – Winnie the Pooh

Ethnicity (ies) – cultural group
   Ex- African American, Haitian, Jewish, Cherokee

Food – traditional food, snack, or drink
   Ex- Cheese & Eggs from Rich Square

Music – sounds, songs, or genres
   Ex- Juke Joint Genre, Rock, Soca

Home – the place you live: sounds, smells, things you see
   Ex- bright colors, ethnic art, incense

Surroundings/Neighborhood – your current natural setting and structure of your immediate space outside of your home. As a child or current
   Ex – Town home community, lots of trees and young families; fields of cotton, corn, tobacco, dirt roads

Race – the racial group or groups you identify with
Ex- Black, White, Latino/Hispanic, Asian, Indian.

First language – the language that was spoken by you in your
home as a child; include dialects
Ex- English, Spanish, Patois

Processing Questions

How did the activity make you feel?

Did you have anything in common with fellow participants? If so, what?

What do you like about the activity?

What did you not like about the activity?

Are we often given time to share these things with each other? Why or why not?

Do you usually ask these questions up front when meeting someone new or when you are developing a work relationship? Why or why not?

Key Points

Take time to learn deeply about one another.

It is important to develop more intentional relationships in order to understand other more.

Be inquisitive after this activity! Seek to learn more about each other.

SOURCES

1. "1819-2013: A History of American Indian Education." Education Week. Web. 01 Jan. 2016.

2. "Campus Demands." The Demands. Web. 01 Jan. 2016.

3. Hill, Lauryn, and Lauryn Hill. Lauryn Hill Mtv Unplugged No. 2.0. Columbia, 2002. CD.

4. Hurston, Lucy Anne. Speak, so You Can Speak Again: The Life of Zora Neale Hurston. New York: Doubleday, 2004. Print.

5. Diplomatic. Merriam-Webster. Merriam-Webster. Web. 05 Jan. 2016.

6. Nice. Merriam-Webster. Merriam-Webster. Web. 01 Apr. 2016.

7. "Sankofa Bird." The Meaning. Web. 01 Dec. 2016.

8. "The Definition of Bold." Dictionary.com. Web. 05 Jan. 2015.

9. "The Meaning of #BlackGirlMagic, And How You Can Get Some Of It." Huffington Post. 2016. Web. 22 Jan. 2016

10. "'What We Want, What We Believe': Teaching with the Black Panthers' Ten Point Program." Zinn Education Project What We Want What We Believe Teaching with the Black Panthers Ten Point Program Comments. 2011. Web. 01 Nov. 2015.

ABOUT THE AUTHOR

Jada Monica Drew is recognized as a United Nations DPINGO – Youth at the Forefront Climate Change speaker, Jada has designed countless diversity and inclusion programs in the public and private sectors for more than a decade. She is the CEO of Social Designs; a social justice consulting firm. Social Designs provides social justice solutions for organizations and people across the globe.

Jada's first book & tour Revolutionize Now is a movement equipping educators, social justice activists, and business leaders with tangible tools for radicalizing systems & evolving self.

Jada has been key in shaping organizations to be more inclusive and equitable in the US, Brazil, El Salvador, Barbados, and Puerto Rico to name a few places. Connecting people and linking their commonalities has been her goal since Drew was young. Her interest in multiculturalism and diversity during undergraduate school started her quest to connect people with the purposes of healing and celebrating differences. Drew holds a master's degree in global and international education with a peace education focus from Drexel University and a bachelor's degree in psychology and minors in African-American studies and education from Guilford College.

Book Jada for executive coaching, consulting, trainings and keynotes.

www.JadaMonicaDrew.com
@jdotdrew
#RevolutionizeNow

Made in the USA
Charleston, SC
05 June 2016